GO DEEPER

"It is rare these days that you find a book that is so saturated with Scripture. *Go Deeper* is a thorough exposition rich in biblical story and tradition. We should applaud the serious nature of this work. It will serve the people of God well in forming them in Christlikeness."

—**BILL HULL**, Author of *The Disciple Making Pastor*,
The Disciple Making Church, and *Choose the Life*

"Through the power of story—God's story and yours—Ken Jung leads us into an enriching discovery of God's distinct attributes. More than that, we are invited to lean fully into experiencing those traits in our daily relationship with the Lord. Explore the Word with this good teacher, and with an open mind and heart you will undoubtedly be led into a fuller knowledge of Almighty God. Enter and *Go Deeper*—you'll be glad you did."

—**STEPHEN A. MACCHIA,** Founder and President of
Leadership Transformations, the Director of the Pierce Center
at Gordon-Conwell Theological Seminary, and
the author of several books, including *Becoming A Healthy Church*
(Baker Books) and *Crafting A Rule of Life* (InterVarsity/Formatio)

"Ken Jung has put together years of insightful analysis into an easy-to-read, yet profound book. At whatever stage of spiritual maturity you find yourself, I highly recommend that you put *Go Deeper* on your list of 'must reads.'"

—**BRETT HILLIARD**, Lead Pastor; Island ECC
(Evangelical Community Church), Hong Kong

Go Deeper richly reveals God's character as He is revealed in the Scriptures. Ken Jung makes the familiar stories of the Bible come alive and more appealing with easy-to-understand presentations on God's attributes. In this book we discover how God relates to us in different ways and situations in life. It's essential in life and ministry to go deep in our theology. *Go Deeper* will serve as a valuable resource for personal spiritual growth and development, small group ministry, and sermon preparation.

—**REV. PRISCO M. ALLOCOD**,
President of the Evangelical Free Church of the Philippines

"A very helpful book, packed with accessible wisdom. The focus on 'story theology' enables Ken to move helpfully between asking questions of the narratives to the narrative asking questions of the reader. His focus throughout is on spiritual formation through real experiences of God. As someone who works with Christians in recovery, I can clearly see how this would ground them in their understanding of the nature of God, in their understanding of the Bible, and being able to relate to what they read to real life situations."

—**STUART LEITCH**, Former Pastor of Alma Church, Bristol, UK; presently working in Christian Addiction Recovery through Crisis Centre Ministries and the Life Recovery Group, Bristol, UK

"As I read *Go Deeper*, I was first captivated by the term 'story theology'. Ken's writing style is engaging and it kept me motivated as he traced some of the familiar stories of Scripture. This book brings new insights into the stories we love and challenges us to go deeper in applying these timeless truths in our own life. Great read!"

—**RON EDMONDSON**, Lead Pastor of Emmanuel Baptist Church, Lexington, Kentucky

"Ken Jung's book *Go Deeper* skillfully uses the Scriptures and points the reader to the major theme of the Bible, the glorious person of God. To read the stories of the Bible and to miss the God behind the stories is to misread the Bible."

—**DR. BILL THRASHER,** Professor; Moody Theological Seminary

"If you want to truly connect other people, you must relate to them at a heart level, at the level of feelings, fears, frustrations, joys, hopes, and aspirations. This is the stuff of stories. *Go Deeper* shows how to mine these priceless elements from both Scripture and real life...and in the process to enjoy deep and exhilarating relationships with both God and the people around you."

—**KEN SANDE,** Founder of Peacemaker Ministries and Relational Wisdom 360

"Dr. Jung's work in this volume is both outstanding and remarkable! I enjoyed reading every word of *Go Deeper* because his storytelling style made Biblical truth come alive and he made it relevant and applicable in my personal life as well as my professional practice. He has succeeded in somehow making these profound relational truths simple and fun to read. I recommend this to all believers as well as seekers!"

—**MELVIN WAIHONG WONG**, Ph.D. California Licensed Psychologist; former Professor of Psychiatry and former Director of the Pastoral Counseling Program, Hong Kong Baptist Theological Seminary

"This is what we long for…to *Go Deeper* with God. It's what we long for those we are discipling…for them to *Go Deeper* with God. Pastor Ken Jung has blessed us with a highly usable, practical tool that challenges us all to grow in the depth of our walk with God as we come to know God through His amazing attributes. Let me urge you strongly to dive in and go deep!"

—**RON KING**, Lead Pastor of Bridges Community Church, Fremont, California

"Every life tells a story and the LORD has chosen to reveal Himself in His Scriptures through lives! Ken Jung draws out these pictures nicely – scripturally saturated, delightfully devotional and wonderfully contemporary – have fun going deeper!"

—**REV CHUA CHUNG KAI**, Chairman of the Evangelical Free Church of Singapore

"Story theology is a compelling, engaging way to encounter the Bible and all of its interactions. This is especially useful for new believers who don't have in-depth knowledge of the Bible or spiritual maturity. *Go Deeper*, by Ken Jung, is an excellent resource and teaching tool. It's evident that Ken has spent countless hours researching and creating this book. I believe this is a very effective way to introduce new believers (and even those who haven't yet made a decision to follow Christ) to the infallible truths found in God's Word."

—**JAMES STEINER**, CEO of Men's Ministry Catalyst

"Every person has a story and making sense of that story requires one to connect with the account of God's gracious work in this world. Ken Jung offers a refreshing look at God's character and challenges each reader to let Scripture form one's life. This book reflects his passion for individuals to *Go Deeper* in relationship with the living God!"

—**DAVID M. JONES, JR.**, Lead Pastor of
Bethel Grove Bible Church, Ithaca, NY

"With insight, passion, and logic, Ken Jung leads us to the one Hero in the Bible's story, God Himself. Filled with Scripture, clear illustrations and careful attention to the Bible's story, *Go Deeper* reads like a 21st century version of *Knowing God*."

—**ROB PENNER**, Pastor and Missionary in East Asia for 25 years

"I encourage you to read *Go Deeper* with a highlighter and an open Bible. Dr. Jung has emphasized the basic fundamentals of the Christian faith in a refreshing way. I hope this works receives a wide reading. Today's church is learning that far from a being a mystical term, spiritual formation is the normative pattern of growth for every believer. Read *Go Deeper* by yourself or with your small group and deepen your walk with Christ!"

—**DR. PAUL PETTIT**, Director of Placement and Adjunct Professor in
Pastoral Ministries and Spiritual Formation, Dallas Theological Seminary

"Story theology is drawing spiritual lessons from some of the narratives in the greatest-of-all storybooks, the Bible. That's what Ken does in *Go Deeper*. Personal examples, helpful summary lists of other Scripture verses relating to the topic of hand, and insightful questions to bring the lessons to a personal level make this a unique and useful book."

—**DAVE AUFRANCE**, Missionary in Hong Kong for 38 years with
Evangelical Friends—Eastern Region and One Mission Society Church
and Pastor of RiverGrace International Christian Fellowship

GO DEEPER

*Encountering
God's Passion*

KEN JUNG

New York

GO DEEPER
Encountering God's Passion

© 2014 KEN JUNG.

Published in New York, New York, by Morgan James Publishing. Morgan James and The Entrepreneurial Publisher are trademarks of Morgan James, LLC. www.MorganJamesPublishing.com

The Morgan James Speakers Group can bring authors to your live event. For more information or to book an event visit The Morgan James Speakers Group at www.TheMorganJamesSpeakersGroup.com.

BitLit
FOR ALL THE BOOKS YOU OWN

FREE eBook edition for your existing eReader with purchase

PRINT NAME ABOVE

For more information, instructions, restrictions, and to register your copy, go to **www.bitlit.ca/readers/register** or use your QR Reader to scan the barcode:

ISBN 978-1-61448-622-0 paperback
ISBN 978-1-61448-623-7 eBook
ISBN 978-1-61448-624-4 audio
ISBN 978-1-61448-885-9 hard cover
Library of Congress Control Number:
2013946289

Cover Design by:
Rachel Lopez
www.r2cdesign.com

Interior Design by:
Bonnie Bushman
bonnie@caboodlegraphics.com

In an effort to support local communities, raise awareness and funds, Morgan James Publishing donates a percentage of all book sales for the life of each book to Habitat for Humanity Peninsula and Greater Williamsburg.

Get involved today, visit
www.MorganJamesBuilds.com

Habitat
for Humanity
Peninsula and
Greater Williamsburg
Building Partner

DEDICATION

To my wife Peggy,
the most gracious servant of all

TABLE OF CONTENTS

ACKNOWLEDGEMENTS

I love stories.

Good stories take us on journeys. My journey of writing *Go Deeper* includes many paths, but the most important ones are spiritual communities, generous families, and amazing friendships. To these three, I wish to express my gratitude.

Thanks to Great Commission Church International, Evangelical Community Church (Hong Kong), Alma Church (Bristol, England), Bethel Grove Bible Church, and Bridges Community Church. Serving, teaching, and leading in a variety of cultural contexts have provided me with rich and diverse experiences.

I'm grateful to United Christian College (secondary school, Hong Kong). Teaching in the ESS (English Speaking Students) program has been one of my greatest joys. Granting me the freedom to use my personality and giftedness enabled me to serve more efficiently.

Like giant sequoias, my parents have provided me with a sense of permanence and stability. Your lives testify to the importance of hard work and hospitality. Thanks to my parents-in-laws for showering us with generosity and support. To Steven (and Wendy), Kevin (and Hilary), Helen, Ivy (and Edwin): May we continue to deepen our relationships.

I've been married to Peggy for eighteen years. I'm still humbled that you chose to be with me. And...I know that I'm a better person for being with you. You have blessed our sons in immeasurable ways! William, we give thanks for your sincerity and faithfulness. Timothy, we appreciate your spontaneity and humor.

No journey would be complete without travel companions. To name just three: To Tom Soong, our twenty-seven years of friendship has been a constant source of encouragement. Much thanks to Jerry Wong for discipling me during my college years. I'm grateful to Wilson Wang for our "Big Three" conversations: theology, ministry, and relationships.

Finally, thanks to the San Diego Christian Writers Guild and Morgan James Publishing. The SDCWG created a platform for me to chase my dreams. Much appreciation to Terry Whalin, Bethany Marshall, Jim Howard, and Lyza Poulin of Morgan James Publishing for helping *Go Deeper* become a reality.

FOREWORD

In his thoughtful and now-classic book, *The Power of Story*, Dr. Leighton Ford explores the idea that effective evangelism is often "narrative evangelism" — that is, people connect with us at the point of our personal experiences and our personal interaction with God. As we tell our own stories of walking with God, Ford explains, others are invited and welcomed into God's presence.

In the pages of his new and important book, *Go Deeper*, Pastor Ken Jung examines another way ("story theology") in which narrative impacts the breadth and depth of our spiritual journeys. Jung argues here that spiritual formation and spiritual deepening are greatly aided by the power of narrative — to transform our lives, to shape our understanding, and to lead us toward qualitative changes in our walk with God.

Jung's point is well taken. In the pages of this carefully organized volume the reader discovers how the exploration of story — God's story, and the stories of God-followers as recorded in Scripture — can have a transformational impact on those who seek to be faithful disciples of Christ.

Lisa and I met Ken at a conference for Christian writers some years ago. It was clear even then that spiritual formation and spiritual deepening are a life focus for this intelligent, articulate servant of God. Having taught, preached and blogged on these topics in a variety of settings — including internationally — Jung now assembles a helpful body of teaching material into this new work.

As a marriage and family counselor, I read many books that deal with interpersonal relationships, parenting and divorce. While *Go Deeper* does not focus on these issues, it will benefit everyone who seeks transformation. Pastors, professors and ministry leaders will find an excellent template here for explaining and exploring spiritual growth and spiritual formation. Students of theology, mentors and new Christians will enjoy the book as well. *Go Deeper* in its broadest sense — is a book for anyone who hungers to know God more deeply, to follow Him more closely, and to honor Him daily in word, thought and deed.

Through insights gained in this book, we can bring our longing for God (Psalm 63) into a new realm of learning, helping us move forward toward maturity in Christ. As we do so, God's story becomes our story, and our story becomes His.

—**Dr. David Frisbie**, The Center for Marriage
& Family Studies, Del Mar, California

INTRODUCTION

Growing up in southern California has its distinct advantages. A lot of people learn to swim because you're never too far away from some body of water. My parents understood this and enrolled us (my brothers and me) in swimming lessons.

The climax of the swimming lessons was jumping off the high dive. I remember watching the big people jumping off the board — it was scary. Now, it was my turn. It took sixty steps (something like that) to get to the top. I slowly made my way to the edge and froze. It was a long way down.

The moment of truth arrived. I simply took a step of faith. I jumped off the high dive. In a split second, I was landing in the water. After you made your big splash, you would *Go Deeper* in the water than you ever went before.

Because you plunged down from the high dive to the bottom of the pool (and lived to tell about it), you knew everything was going to be all right. You were now confident enough to swim in the deep end of the swimming pool. A different world opened up for you (you could go deeper to get those underwater rings).

When I was in my late elementary school years, our family added a swimming pool to our backyard. Those summers were glorious. We were in the pool every day. We invented all kinds of games and had our friends and neighbors over for a swim throughout the summer.

A few years later, we got a motor home. During my teen years, we visited different beaches for a week at a time, while on summer vacations. We also had great food as my dad — a barbecue kind of a dad — would cook food like steak and fish. We ate like kings! And this was way before the *Food Network*!

One of the great things about the beach is that you can *Go Deeper*. You didn't have to worry about the edge of the swimming pool or being limited by an eight-and-a-half foot deep end. I could use the boogey board or body surf in the waves at the beach. The farther and deeper you went, however, the more mysterious the beach became. The waves were higher and more powerful. Near the shore, they seemed calm and refreshing. Going deeper challenged my comfort zone!

Like the beach, God can also be mysterious. What's God like? Am I taking a risk if I choose to *Go Deeper*? Absolutely! When it comes to deepening our spiritual intimacy with God — "the greater the risk, the greater the reward" is a rule that definitely applies.

Go Deeper is about a passionate God, who has been pursuing us…

Go Deeper is about a passionate God, who has been pursuing us ever since we were born. So, it's not a book that will merely teach us about God's sovereignty, holiness, and grace, for instance. Rather, it's a book that encourages us to encounter and experience a sovereign, holy, and gracious God.

Go Deeper also focuses on spiritual formation. What is spiritual formation? Let me share five thoughts. (1) Spiritual formation is the intentional process by which the Spirit develops Christ's character. We become more like Christ in thoughts, desires, words, and actions.

(2) Spiritual formation does not occur in a straight and linear line of development. Because our past experiences and sinful habits are difficult to overcome, Christ-followers experience ups and downs, doubt, anxiety, peaks and valleys.

(3) Because human beings are composed of material and immaterial entities (Genesis 2:7; Matthew 10:28; 2 Corinthians 4:16; James 2:26), spiritual formation must take into consideration both elements. We have a soul and we have a body. We also function as holistic creatures; our souls affect our bodies and our bodies affect our souls. Our brokenness is not just spiritual, but it's physical as well. Christ came to make us spiritually and physically whole. Throughout *Go Deeper*, I will use the phrase, "body and soul," to refer to our dualistic nature and holistic function.[1]

(4) Since spiritual formation is holistic, we don't just read the Bible, sing worship songs, and pray to God, but we also need to serve others, persevere through trials, sacrifice financially, take risks, and fulfill our calling. (5) Spiritual formation is intentional. It won't "just happen," but rather, Christ-followers will be transformed because both the Spirit and Christ-followers play an active role. This means that we will need to live disciplined lives in order to experience transformation (1 Corinthians 9:24-27).

There are ten chapters in *Go Deeper*. "What Is Story Theology?" (chapter 1) is the foundation for the book. I explain how Christ-followers come to know and deepen their relationship with God. I draw attention to the importance of the biblical narratives and characters as models for our spiritual formation. Because story theology is the matrix for most of these chapters (3 through 10), it's important to understand this approach to Scripture.

Story theology draws from the insights of theology and literature. Concerning theology, I list several Bible verses in bullet-point form throughout *Go Deeper*. Don't be intimidated by these lists! Because Scripture plays such an important role spiritual formation, I wanted you to have the whole counsel of God's Word. At times, some of these lists will read like a "textbook." Hang in there! Read slowly. Reflect on these verses. My prayer is for you to understand and experience the beauty of these biblical truths.

My writing style also highlights the importance of narrative. Each chapter includes an introduction and background section for understanding the historical and social context for each biblical character. I also use four "voices" in the exposition sections to help you experience the character's thoughts and feelings. (1) Direct quotes from the Scripture have quotation marks with biblical references. (2) The imagined script spoken by the biblical characters is identified with quotation marks without biblical references. (3) The stage direction imported from the biblical narrative has brackets. (4) My interjected questions and comments are italicized.

Chapters 2 through 10 highlight one (sometimes two) of God's attributes. Although each chapter focuses on a primary attribute, we should remember that God possesses all of these attributes together. I have selected one biblical character for each chapter to assist us on our spiritual journey. By focusing on a character, we will observe how God transformed this person's life (the creation story is the only exception). So, what kind of God will you encounter?

In chapter 2, God's awesome power and eternal nature are on display in the creation story (Genesis 1). You will discover what it means when we say, "God is majestic." The next story declares God's judgment. God's role as a judge is in full view with Adam and Eve (chapter 3). You will also learn hope. God's sovereignty is proclaimed through the life of Joseph in chapter 4. Imprisoned for a crime he didn't commit, see what happens to a person who embraces God's plan for his life.

Chapter 5 is about a holy God pursuing a man named Moses. This God calls Moses to liberate His people. God's justice and redemptive community take center stage in Naomi's life (chapter 6). Exchanging her name "Pleasant" for "Bitter," she returns to her faith community. Chapter 7 draws attention to God's grace. Physically broken and living in a barren land, Mephibosheth is victoriously invited to the king's table.

God's omniscience (He knows everything) and omnipresence (He is everywhere present) are highlighted in Elijah's life (chapter 8).

Experiencing exhaustion and depression, he is restored by a "gentle whisper." In chapter 9, God's immutability (He doesn't change) and faithfulness provide strength for Queen Esther, who puts her life on the line for her people. God's love is the focus of chapter 10. Based on a parable taught by Jesus, you will encounter the Father's love for both of His prodigal sons. In short, *Go Deeper* is about a God who pursues us in order to transform us.

Ken Jung
August 2013

Whom have I in heaven but you?
　And there is nothing on earth that I desire besides you.
My flesh and my heart may fail,
　but God is the strength of my heart and my portion forever.
　　　　　　　　　　　　　　　　　　　　– Psalm 73:25–26

CHAPTER 1

WHAT IS STORY THEOLOGY?

Introduction

The word "theology" means the study of God. Any attempt to study God, however, brings many questions, doesn't it? Here are several. How can finite human beings understand an infinite and mysterious God? Should our investigation be limited to only the Christian Scriptures as the source for theology? Should we include natural theology in our study? How can spiritual experiences help us study God?

If we were studying a specific fish or bird we might have an idea about how to do it, but how do we go about studying God? How long must we study God in order to know Him? Do I need to go to a Bible college, seminary, or attend a weekly Bible study to know God? Or, what about finding some spiritual teacher? Do I need a spiritual mentor to know God?

Another issue related to studying God concerns our attitude. For many, theology is a boring and futile exercise for knowing God. In contrast to these attitudes, Tozer in *The Knowledge of the Holy*, proclaims: "The study of the attributes of God, far from being dull and heavy, may...be a sweet

1

and absorbing spiritual exercise. To the soul that is athirst for God, nothing could be more delightful."[2]

Who Is God?

I'm going to ask you a question, but you can't ask someone else for the answer. Ready? "Who is God?" Or to put it another way: "What is God like?" Before you answer either of these questions, I want you to consider the first two steps in looking for the answer. After you complete steps 1 and 2, then we will meet at a coffee shop for a conversation about God.

So, what's your first step? My guess is that many people would probably go directly to the Bible. That's the best place to begin. The Bible clearly teaches a lot about God's character. Which Bible passages would you look up? Would they be verses like "Consecrate yourselves therefore, and be holy for I am holy….You shall therefore be holy, for I am holy" (Leviticus 11:44–45) and "God is love" (1 John 4:8)? Or would you find a story in the Bible to answer the question "Who is God?"

What's step 2? Some of you would find a book about God's attributes. What about Kay Arthur's *The Power of Knowing God*, A.W. Pink's *The Attributes of God*, A.W. Tozer's, *The Knowledge of the Holy*, and J.I. Packer's *Knowing God*? Have you read any of these books? Which book — not limited to the ones listed above — would you recommend to a friend who wants to know God?

Perhaps, you have a Bible college or seminary background? If so, you might have reached for Wayne Grudem's *Systematic Theology*, Louis Berkhof's *Systematic Theology*, John Calvin's *The Institutes of the Christian Religion*, Millard Erickson's *Christian Theology*, or J. Rodham Williams's *Renewal Theology*. Do any of these books sound familiar? Do you have a preference for one of these books?

In brief, in attempting to answer the question "Who is God?", many Christians cite propositions (God is holy, God is love), Bible verses (Leviticus 11:44–45, 1 John 4:8), or their favorite book. It has been said that the primary purpose of Christ-followers is to know God and make Him known. If we are to pursue this purpose, then we need to know God.

How Do We Come to Know God?

God wants a dynamic relationship with us — this cannot be denied. However, it's also true that most of the people in the world do not have a personal relationship with Him. Consider the people who make up your world — I don't mean those who attend your church or small group community.

Most of those around us (colleagues, neighbors, classmates) and those in different careers (bankers, bakers, teachers, doctors, lawyers, electricians, police officers, grocers, managers, and engineers) do not have a relationship with God. Have you thought about the reasons why this is so? Let me share three observations about knowing God.

Observation #1: Sin Stops Us from Knowing God

Sin may be defined in many ways. For our discussion, I will focus on two areas. First, sin is transgressing or breaking God's perfect and moral standard. The Apostle John tells us that "everyone who makes a practice of sinning also practices lawlessness; sin is lawlessness" (1 John 3:4). Thus, in our desires, thoughts, words, and actions we break God's moral standard.

Committing sin is like a person who reads a sign DO NOT LITTER, ignores the sign, and purposely throws his candy wrappers, napkins, and other pieces of trash blatantly on the street. In other words, committing sin is willfully disobeying God's moral standard.

How does this understanding of sin affect our ability to be in a relationship with God? We live for ourselves. When we do so, we have moved from a theocentric to an egocentric worldview by dethroning God and placed ourselves at the center.

Rather than worshiping, loving, and serving God, we have become our own gods and we live for our own purposes and desires. Sin has created a spiritual vacuum in our lives. It has alienated us from God and caused us to seek ultimate satisfaction through human relationships, materialism, careers, physical appearance, cars, and homes.

Second, sin refers to missing the mark of God's perfect standard. Romans 3:23 reflects this idea: "For all have sinned and fall short of the glory of God." Like novice archers taking aim at the target for the first time, we have all missed the bull's-eye! Actually, sin is worse than that: With sin, *every time* we shoot our arrow, we miss the bull's-eye.

Sometimes, our arrow may hit closer to the bull's-eye, but we always miss the target and fall short of God's perfect standard. From a practical standpoint of knowing God, this means that our efforts of knowing Him fall short because we try to reach God through our own efforts via religion, spirituality, service, and morality.

Observation #2: Knowledge of God is not Equivalent to Knowing God

I know a person named John. John is six feet tall and weighs one hundred and ninety pounds. He was born in Asia, has black hair, brown eyes, speaks two languages, graduated from university with a major in comparative literature, married in the year of 2002, and works as a high school teacher. I could tell you what he likes to eat, his favorite vacation destinations, if he exercises or not, and much more. Knowing these facts alone, however, is not the same as knowing John personally.

Similarly, to know God is more than acknowledging that something or someone created our universe or our world. Knowing God is more than defining His attributes — God is eternal, sovereign, holy, gracious, all-powerful, all-knowing, present everywhere, and loving. To know that God loves justice, mercy, and humility is not the same as having a personal relationship with Him either. In fact, we could memorize hundreds of Bible verses and recite them perfectly and yet still not know God in a dynamic and personal way.

Observation #3: Knowing God is Based on a Relationship with Jesus

To know God is to be in a personal relationship with Him.[3] Drawing from the Old Testament symbol of the tabernacle, the Apostle John declared that Jesus was God's tabernacle — full of truth and grace, revealed in human flesh (John 1:14). He came to give us the opportunity to live a full and meaningful life (John 10:10). Many people, however, do not have a personal relationship with God because of our spiritual condition.

Our spiritual condition is one of separation. We are separated from God; we need to be forgiven for our sins and reconciled to God. Salvation and forgiveness is based on Jesus's death on the cross and resurrection from the dead. In his death, Jesus paid the penalty for our sins (Romans 6:23) and became a substitution for our sins (Romans 5:21). In his resurrection, Jesus conquered sin and death (Romans 6:1-14; 8:1-17; 1 Corinthians 15:55-57).

We come to know God through a personal relationship with Jesus, His Son (John 17:3). Jesus Himself proclaimed this: "I am the way, and the truth, and the life. No one comes to the Father except through me. If you had known me, you would have known my Father also. From now on you do know him and have seen him." (John 14:6-7) We establish a relationship with Jesus by believing that only He can save us from our sins (John 3:16). We make a commitment to follow Jesus for the rest of our life (Mark 8:34-38).

After Jesus resurrected from the dead, He called His apostles to make disciples of all nations (Matthew 28:19–20). This call to discipleship — the first step being evangelism — is reflected in the Early Church's proclamation of the gospel. The book of Acts testifies to this truth several times (2:38; 4:12; 5:30–31; 10:42–43; 13:38–39; 16:31).

In addition, the New Testament shows a pattern of devotion to Christ. This pattern of devotion includes spiritual practices such as praying to Jesus (Acts 7:59), baptism in His name (Matthew 28:19–20), partaking in the Lord's Supper (1 Corinthians 11:23-32), and singing hymns to Christ (Ephesians 5:19).[4] These spiritual practices help us to develop our relationship with Jesus.

Let me summarize: We come to know God through establishing a spiritual relationship with Jesus. Having been forgiven of our sins and reconciled to the Father, we are now children of God (John 1:12), children who devote themselves to following, worshiping, and serving Jesus.

Go Deeper in the Word (Part 1)

After establishing a relationship with God in Jesus, we then begin to deepen our relationship with God through two primary elements: The

Ministry of the Word and Spirit. For my discussion on God's Word, I will share three principles.

Principle #1: Make Scripture a Priority (Deuteronomy 6:4–9)

Life under the Torah was a lifestyle that was saturated with the Scriptures from morning to evening and from place to place. As people walked and traveled throughout the day, their traveling companions included God's Word.[5]

The Scriptures were also symbols on their bodies and homes so that the Word of God surrounded their physical and everyday activities in both private and public spheres. All of these examples point to the fact that God's people have been called to make the Word of God a priority in their lives regardless of their busyness.

Principle #2: Christians Renew Their Minds with Scripture (Romans 12:1–2; 2 Corinthians 10:1–6; cf. John 17:13–19; Hebrews 4:12–13)

Romans 12:1–2 highlights the significance of a renewed mind. Our thought life plays a pivotal role in spiritual formation. The mind acts as a gatekeeper of knowledge and helps us to apply our ideas into everyday living. Because we are fallen creatures our minds need to be renewed and spiritually transformed by God's Word.

In 2 Corinthians 10:1–6, Paul addresses those in Corinth to take captive every thought to Christ in light of the false beliefs and teachings. Using the Scriptures as our guide, Paul is calling us to bring our thought life and patterns under the Lordship of Jesus.

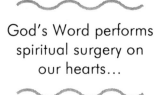

God's Word performs spiritual surgery on our hearts…

In John 17:13–19, Jesus claims that God's Word sanctifies us in truth. How can truth make us holy? Because the Scriptures are true; they can protect us from the lies of the world. According to Hebrews 4:12–13, the spiritual sword penetrates the spiritual flesh of human beings "discerning the thoughts and attentions of the heart." God's Word performs spiritual surgery on our hearts in order to spiritually form us into Christ's image.

Principle #3: Christ-Followers Should Mediate on Scripture (Joshua 1:6–9; Psalm 1; Colossians 3:15–17)

The idea of Christian meditation refers to the spiritual practice of reflecting on the nature and importance of a biblical truth. In Joshua 1:6–9, God tells Joshua that meditating on God's law day and night was the key to obeying His law. Psalm 1 compares the life of the wicked and righteous. The fruit of the righteous that was planted by "streams of water" was a result of delighting and meditating on God's law. Regarding Colossians 3:15–17, dwelling on the Word of God brings peace in the midst of strife and anxiety.

Go Deeper in the Spirit (Part 2)

When a person becomes a Christian, they receive the Holy Spirit — we become God's temple and the Spirit lives within us (1 Corinthians 6:19). We may understand the Spirit's role in our lives by highlighting three roles: (1) personal ministries of the Spirit; (2) the fruit of the Spirit; and (3) gifts of the Spirit.

Role #1: The Spirit Is the Key to Spiritual Formation

The Spirit has sanctified us — made us holy so that we can succeed in being more like Christ and serving God (Romans 15:16). Jesus called the Spirit our helper (John 14:16). He testifies to and glorifies Jesus (John 15:26). The Spirit teaches, convicts us of sin, and reveals truth (John 14:26; 16:8, 13).

The Holy Spirit also leads, strengthens, encourages, and empowers us for holiness and service (Romans 8:14; 9:31; Ephesians 5:18). The Spirit bears witness with our spirit that we are children of God. Concerning prayer, He intercedes for us when we are too weak (Romans 8:26). On the other hand, we can resist (Acts 7:51) and quench the Spirit's work within us (1 Thessalonians 5:19). Our disobedience also grieves the Spirit (Ephesians 4:30).

Role #2: The Spirit Produces Christ-Like Character

Our purpose is to be like Jesus — in thoughts, desires, words, and actions. This process is called spiritual formation, the intentional process by which the Spirit develops Christ's character. By following Christ, we develop the "fruit of the Spirit," traits such as "love, joy, peace, patience, kindness, goodness, faithfulness, gentleness, and self-control" begin to develop in our lives (Galatians 5:22–23) The Spirit transforms us from the inside out. This inner transformation helps us to deal with issues such as personal identity, bitterness, destructive behavior patterns, pride, and materialism.

Role #3: The Spirit Gives Us Spiritual Gifts to Edify and Serve Other Christians (Romans 12:6–8; 1 Corinthians 12:4–11, 28–31; 1 Peter 4:10)

Although there is a diversity of spiritual gifts, we are unified in the Body of Christ because there is only one universal spiritual body that all Christians — past, present, future — belong to.[6] Christians are called to use their spiritual gifts in love to serve others — not for selfish promotion or gain. In addition, we use our spiritual gifts naturally and passionately. For instance, not only do I naturally enjoy teaching the Scriptures and providing leadership, but I am also passionate about these kinds of activities as well.

Personal Experiences with God: Three Traits

Our personal experiences with God are a result of the ministry of the Word and Spirit in our lives. Let me illustrate this with a story about Stacy and Liza. As the years pass, Stacy and Liza deepen their personal relationship in many ways. For instance, they communicate by listening to one another and sharing their fears, joys, hurts, and dreams. They spend time together eating, shopping, and traveling. Liza and Stacy enjoy one another's presence. Their relationship didn't just happen overnight — it took many months.

Like Liza and Stacy's relationship, God desires for us to have a deeper relationship with Him. Throughout Scripture, God's people had many personal experiences that brought them into a more intimate relationship with Him. While these experiences varied, all of them had three traits in common — these spiritual experiences were real, theological, and transforming.

Real Experiences

What do I mean by real experiences? Not only were Joseph, Moses, and Esther's experiences of God not illusionary, but they left such a deep impression that they were undeniably real. Here are some other undeniably real examples: I can see pictures on my wall, feel hot water as I drink it out of my mug, and hear the television in the family room. Unless I am physically or psychologically impaired, my senses inform me of these undeniably real experiences.

Joseph experienced God through his hardships, Moses experienced God through a burning bush, and Esther experienced God when He delivered her people from extermination. These were undeniably real *spiritual experiences*. Joseph, Moses, and Esther did not doubt nor were skeptical about these experiences with God.

They were real experiences because God impressed upon these biblical characters the genuineness and truthfulness of these spiritual experiences. God clearly revealed to these people that they were experiencing the living God! Let me unpack this idea of real experiences with one additional insight.

Some experiences can be fleeting. It's not that they didn't happen, but rather, that they are less significant in our lives. For instance, when I wake up in the morning I have a real experience of brushing my teeth. It really does happen seven days a week!

I would classify this experience of brushing my teeth as fleeting because the experience passes quickly until I brush my teeth again. Joseph, Moses, and Esther, on the other hand, had real experiences with God that were so meaningful and significant that they left an enduring and long-lasting mark on their lives.

Theological Experiences

These experiences of Joseph, Moses, and Esther were enduring and long lasting because they were theological experiences. These experiences were not based on a person's sense experience of static and inanimate objects like desks, trees, and skyscrapers. Experiences from these objects would include the different sizes, shapes, and colors.

In contrast, theological experiences may be classified as a person-to-person experience. To be more specific, they are called theological experiences because Joseph, Moses, and Esther had personal encounters with the God of the universe, the creator of the heavens and earth.

Joseph, Moses, and Esther's theological experiences were radically different from sitting at the feet of a rabbi or prominent biblical scholar of today. While it's true that they experienced God through the Scriptures, their personal encounters with God must have been an altogether different way of experiencing Him.

To encounter God firsthand must have been an awe-inspiring, jaw-dropping, one-of-a-kind experience. In a word, these personal experiences with God were transcendent experiences. They surpassed the normal, everyday experiences of sight, smell, sound, taste, and touch.

Because life does not occur in an empty vacuum, Joseph, Moses, and Esther experienced God in the midst of their fears, hopes, sorrow, and joy. As pilgrims on a spiritual journey, they encountered God in many different ways. While not negating or losing any of His attributes, a particular attribute of God's character would be experienced in a deeper way.

Joseph, for instance, experienced God's sovereignty through being sold by his brothers, imprisoned, starved, and reunited with his family. Moses experienced God's holiness while communicating with God through a burning bush. Esther experienced God's immutability and faithfulness when He delivered her people from genocide.

I'm also referring to these experiences of Joseph, Moses, and Esther as theological because we can understand biblical truth from these experiences. This is not to say that all our experiences of God are necessarily "theological." Let me explain. Because Joseph, Moses, and Esther's experiences are recorded for us in God's Word, they have His authority and reflect His written revelation of truth.

On the other hand, if you or I have a religious experience that does not find unity and consistency with God's Word, then we should hesitate to refer to it as a theological experience. In short, the

> ...the experiences of Joseph, Moses, and Esther shaped and formed their theology as well as ours.

experiences of Joseph, Moses, and Esther shaped and formed their theology as well as ours.

Transforming Experiences

Joseph, Moses, and Esther's personal encounters with God were not only real and theological experiences, but they were transforming ones as well. Can you imagine the thoughts and emotions that Joseph must have had in light of his circumstances? For instance, how did it feel to be betrayed by your very own brothers and sold to a traveling caravan heading to Egypt? What kind of God allows a person to be imprisoned for doing the right thing — fleeing from sexual temptation?

As Joseph was on his way toward Egypt and languishing in prison, God was slowly transforming him through these unfair and seemingly impossible circumstances. God was shaping Joseph through these hardships so that he could trust in His sovereign hand. It was God — and not the Pharaoh or even Joseph — who was in control.

We can testify to the same truth for Moses and Esther as well. Moses's experience of communicating with God through a burning bush radically transformed him in several ways. First, Moses was transformed in his understanding of God's nature. He realized that not only was God absolutely pure and morally righteous, but that He was totally set apart from all living or nonliving things.

Second, Moses was transformed in his understanding of human nature. He experienced in a deeper way that he was sinful. Third, Moses was transformed in his worship and service for God. God alone — not the

Pharaoh — deserved to receive glory, honor, and praise. The Israelites were not called to serve at the Pharaoh's bidding, but called to serve a holy God.

Esther's experience of being delivered from the hands of Haman transformed her too. Let me share a few thoughts. First, Esther was transformed by God's grace. Esther's rise to a place of privilege and honor as the queen was God's gift to her and the Jewish nation. It was solely an act of God's unmerited favor bestowed upon Esther.

Second, Esther was transformed by God's protection. Delivering the Jews from extermination, God came alongside of His people and fought for them and defeated their enemy. It's not a surprise that the Feast of Purim celebrates God's protection of Esther and her people.

Third, Esther was transformed by God's justice. Throughout the story, Haman holds all the cards and stays one step ahead of the king. However, Haman's plot is uncovered and he was executed on the very gallows designed for Mordecai. Justice was served!

Doing Story Theology[7]

In light of the ministry of God's Word and Spirit, many of God's people had unique experiences with Him. Some of these have been recorded for us in the Scriptures. In these biblical stories, we catch a glimpse of people being passionately pursued by God.

God pursues people because He wants to transform people, to change their communities and world via the power of the gospel. We have story after story highlighting God's passion for pursuing His people.

I believe that people enjoy stories for one simple reason. We enjoy stories because we can relate to them. We empathize with them. A good story is a story that invites people to place themselves into the story. It's a narrative that moves our emotions, teases our mind, challenges our values, captures our imagination, or inspires us to live differently. Stories appear in all

> The first and greatest storyteller of them all is God Himself.

shapes and sizes — the stage, cinema, television, or books, but they were present first in the words of a storyteller.

The first and greatest storyteller of them all is God Himself. Throughout Scripture, God weaves together many different stories to form a coherent vision. Some of these stories are short while others are long. While there are many things to look for in a story, I want to suggest six action points for doing story theology.

Action Point #1: Consider your life in light of the biblical themes embedded in the story

The theme of Adam and Eve's story in Genesis 3, for example, is God's judgment of sin. When we read this story we can learn three things about our life in relation to God's judgment. First, God's judgment shows that sin will not go unpunished. For God to not judge sin is not an act of love. Rather it's an unjust act. Second, God's judgment is a death declaration. This judgment includes physical death and spiritual death — being separated from God. Third, God's judgment includes an opportunity for mercy. God providing animal skin — an animal must die in order to have its skin for Adam and Eve — is a future symbol of our need for forgiveness through Jesus. In short, Adam and Eve's story asks us to relate God's judgment to our sin and need of forgiveness.

Action Point #2: Reflect on your spiritual journey in relation to the biblical characters

The story of Naomi, for instance, includes all kinds of hurts and pains — emotional, social, and spiritual. Naomi has emotional pain because she has lost her husband and two sons. She also had to deal with social pain because she would have been viewed differently as a widow, especially being a Jew living in Moab.

Naomi had spiritual pain because she struggled with God's hand taking away her husband and two sons. In brief, Naomi's story helps us personally or helps us minister to another person who has experienced bitterness at the hands of God — and yet was transformed in the process. Naomi calls us into action — to look around and serve others even in the midst of our own bitterness and pain.

Action Point #3: Although we are on a spiritual journey, we should not lose sight of our destination

Joseph's life illustrates this point. Joseph was learning about God's sovereignty while being sold to a traveling caravan and unjustly imprisoned. However, he also knew about God's promises (those dreams about his brother's bowing down to him, for example). It's probably true that he didn't understand the full extent of these dreams, but Joseph had faith that his ultimate destination would not be in a prison (see Genesis 50:20).

While doing story theology requires us to reflect on our spiritual journey, we need to remember that we are moving toward a *destination*. It's not all about the journey! We need to consider living and being shaped by God in light of His goal or prize (1 Corinthians 9:24–27). Finishing the race — a marathon for instance — should impact the way I eat, sleep, train, and run in the race itself.

Action Point #4: Use your imagination to understand amazing experiences

Consider the prophet Elijah for a moment. God called him to confront King Ahab and then sent him to a ravine to be fed by ravens. Then, upon meeting a widow, he witnessed her son's death and raised him from the dead. Returning to Israel, Elijah confronted the false prophets of Baal and called down fire from heaven to consume a sacrifice drenched with water.

Running from Jezebel, he wandered through a wilderness and wished himself dead. Awakened and fed by an angel, Elijah finds himself at the mouth of a cave where God reveals Himself in a gentle whisper as opposed to a wind, earthquake, and fire. When it's time for Elijah to depart this earth, he doesn't die but is taken away in a whirlwind.

I count six amazing experiences for the prophet Elijah! Can you relate to any of them? I find it rather difficult myself. Should we reject them or push them aside? What should we do with these amazing experiences?

Imagination. Use your imagination. Stories were also written so that we can imagine the unexpected. God is in the business of doing things beyond our wildest imagination. Take a step back. Be still. Stand in awe of God's majesty, power, and glory. Now imagine — it's really that simple.

Action Point #5: Story theology is about God's story

Having highlighted the importance of locating ourselves in these biblical stories, themes, and characters, we need to remember that story theology is ultimately a God story. To neglect to see God's character in these stories is to misread these stories. This is an important point because we need to guard against the temptation to read these narratives too egotistically.

Story theology is about discovering a God who pursues us in order to have a passionate and dynamic relationship with us. Chip Ingram observes this importance: "We want to encounter, embrace, and know God as he is. And here's the motivation; until you know God as he is, you'll never become all that he's created you to be."[8] Behind these narratives are stories of a God who wants to spiritually transform us so that we fulfill our callings and make Him known.

> Story theology is also Trinitarian.

Story theology is also Trinitarian. While these narratives help us understand and experience God, they ultimately point to Jesus Himself. The redemptive community that Naomi experiences and grace that Mephibosheth experiences point to our spiritual community and grace found in Christ. In addition, the Spirit plays a key role in these stories because He teaches us truth, convicts us of sin, and empowers us for daily living. It is through the Scriptures and Spirit that we are being transformed.

Every chapter in this book identifies one (or two) attributes of God. In the midst of our daily lives — our struggles, victories, hopes, fears, and joys, it's God who is relentless in His pursuit of us. For example, if we are living in sin, God pursues us with His holiness. If our lives are spinning out of control and filled with chaos, God pursues us with His sovereignty.

Action Point #6: Make their stories become our stories — we become storytellers

Being a 2.5 generation American-born Chinese, I didn't experience a lot of Chinese culture growing up. My parents purposely raised us as Americans. When I had the opportunity to visit Beijing, however, I had this amazing experience of being part of this great Chinese tradition as I was standing in The Forbidden City.

Likewise, when we read the Old Testament, Christians tend to think of these stories as stories for God's people in the Old Testament — and not stories for New Testament Christians. Galatians 3:6–9 teaches, however, that we are spiritual children of Abraham. How do you approach the Old Testament narratives? Do you see them as only religious or ethical stories for practical application? Or, do you rejoice because the Old Testament is also our spiritual history too?

Worship service is one of the best contexts for good storytelling. Let me share four practical suggestions. (1) Sermons should include storytelling. We need to help people understand who they are, where they are, and where they are going in light of God's grand narrative. How do people fit into God's plan of creation, fall, redemption, transformation, and consummation? Our preaching should include stories of grace, despair, hope, pain, joy, fear, and perseverance.

(2) Christ-followers become storytellers during worship services (and fellowship groups) by sharing their testimonies. We should encourage Christians to share testimonies of how God has been transforming us. We should testify to God's work in our lives — He receives the glory and praise for helping us to be more like Christ. (Storytelling should not be limited to worship service. Storytellers are created whenever we testify to God's transforming work.)

(3) We also become storytellers through performing drama. Dramas are a good way for the community of faith to "see, hear, and feel" God's stories.

If you don't have the resources for a drama, then consider storytelling by playing short video clips (1–2 minutes in duration) during the service.

(4) Communion also provides a context for storytelling. Rather than serving communion the same way each time, churches should consider different ways of proclaiming the blessings of the Lord's Supper. For instance, we can have people come forward to dip the bread in the cup while leaders proclaim to each person their forgiveness or spiritual identity ("You're a child of God").

We can create multiple stations for taking communion throughout the sanctuary. At these stations, we could have truths such as "Christ died for your sins," "You are dearly loved and forgiven," and "You are alive in Christ" on signs proclaiming the story of the cross.

Another way of taking communion at these stations is to have a large blank sheet of paper and pen. We ask people to write one word to describe their present thoughts or feelings as they are partaking in communion. These lists of words then become part of the storytelling of communion.

Story theology is not limited to worship service. In fact, story theology can be used in all kinds of ministries including evangelism, discipleship, small groups, counseling, and Christian education. We are storytellers when we share the gospel, spiritually invest in other Christians, develop spiritual communities, encourage our Christian brothers and sisters, and equip God's people for life and service. In summary, story theology is not just a different approach to reading Scriptures and spiritual formation, but it's also a way of "doing" ministry and life.

SUMMARY

1. Who is God? For many Christians, we find the answer to this question in two ways. First, we cite propositions or doctrines like "God is love" and "God is holy." Second, we read books — popular and academic — about God's attributes.

2. Knowledge of God is not equivalent to knowing God. We come to know God through having a relationship with Jesus.

3. Drawing insights from the biblical stories and characters, we learn that we go deeper in our relationship with God through the ministry of the Word and Spirit.

4. At times, these biblical characters had spiritual experiences as a result of seeking God. These spiritual experiences have three traits: they are real, theological, and transforming.

5. Doing story theology includes several aspects. We reflect on our spiritual journey in light of the story's theme and character. In addition to the spiritual journey, it's imperative that we do not lose sight of our destination. Also, we use our imagination to understand amazing experiences. Furthermore, story theology is a story about God — He's the main character. Finally, we learn the stories and become storytellers ourselves.

REFLECTION

1. A friend asks you to teach him or her to know God. What kind of advice would you give?

2. How do the Spirit and Word help us to know God in a deep and intimate way? Explain the process.

3. To what extent have you had real, theological, or transforming spiritual experiences? Share your insights with one of your Christian friends.

4. Would "doing story theology" make a difference in your reading of the Scriptures? How would practicing story theology affect your life? Explain.

PRAYER FOR SPIRITUAL FORMATION

Dear God,

As I read *Go Deeper*, I ask for your Spirit to convict me of sin. Empower me for your glory. I know that you are passionately seeking me. You desire intimacy. I want to seek you with all of my heart. Father, help me to see you for who you really are. As I read your Word, let me experience your sovereignty, holiness, presence, grace, and love. Use the Scriptures to transform me. Renew me.

CHAPTER 2

CREATION
Genesis 1:1–31

God's Power and Eternal Nature

Introduction

"So, what's behind the Big Bang?" I inquired.[9] I was in the middle of a discussion about the origin of our universe.

"What does science teach, John?" John was an agnostic and believed that it was impossible to reconcile science with Christianity. John went on to inform me that science doesn't ask questions before the first moment in our universe.

"That's an interesting position, John. May I ask a few questions?" John nodded in affirmation.

I drew a line on the left side of a piece a paper from top to bottom. "This line represents the Big Bang — the first moment in our universe." It looked like a Y axis. Then, to represent time from the first moment until now, I drew an arrow from the bottom left point to the right side on the bottom of the page (this looked like an X axis). Pointing at the line representing the Big Bang, I again asked, "So, what's before this moment in time?" John answered that we don't know or nothing was before the Big Bang.

"John, was the Big Bang a powerful event?"

"Yes."

"Okay, according to what we know about the law of cause and effect, may we say that every created entity fits this cause and effect law?"

John paused. He knew that I was trying to steer him toward a particular direction. "Well, in general that's probably true, Ken."

I continued. "Okay, so if this cause and effect law is true, and the Big Bang was a powerful event, then it's probably true that what caused it must have been powerful, right?"

Without hesitation, John replied, "I know what you're trying to say. But we can't say God."

"Isn't this a fair assumption, John?"

John didn't want to move an inch. "Perhaps, we do, perhaps we don't. We can't say, Ken."

"John, you just informed me that the law of cause and effect applies to created entities. If the Big Bang is an example of a created entity, then it's probably true that something powerful created it. That's all I am saying."

"Okay, Ken. For argument's sake, something powerful may be beyond the Big Bang. However, since science cannot observe the moment before the Big Bang, then we are left to speculate only."

"John, there are degrees of speculations, right?" We both managed a small smile. "Let's look at a few options here." I wrote down the words "self-creation," "nothing," and "something else." "We know the Big Bang didn't create itself. We also know that the Big Bang didn't come from nothing. So, we are left with the option of something else."

I then took my pencil and pointed again to the Y axis. "John, this something else is probably eternal." After my pause, John confidently replied, "Ken, we simply don't know." Realizing that my time was short I attempted to wrap it up.

"John, I'll leave you with three ideas to consider. First, this something is powerful because it's the cause of the Big Bang. Second, this something is probably eternal because it exists outside of our universe and prior to the Big Bang. Third, the two traits of being powerful and eternal reflect a creator God."

John seemed a bit more interested: "Ken, even if this is true — all you have is a deistic God."[10]

I think my final response caught John off guard. "John, you're exactly right. I've only pointed us in the direction of a God who created our universe and world. So far, this is the God of Genesis 1, who is powerful and eternal."

In my conversation with John, I only wanted to focus on the traits of eternity and power. Although all of God's attributes make Him great, these two attributes of God provide reasons for proclaiming His greatness.[11]

Background

The word "majestic" means great. Thus, when we say, "God is majestic," we are proclaiming that He is great. In fact, the word great doesn't do justice to God's majesty. God is supremely great! The Bible declares God's greatness throughout the Scriptures:

- Exodus 15:7, "In the greatness of your majesty you overthrow your adversaries."
- Exodus 15:11, "Who is like you, O LORD, among the gods? Who is like you, majestic in holiness, awesome in glorious deeds, doing wonders?"
- Deuteronomy 33:26, "There is none like God, O Jeshurun, who rides through the heavens to your help, through the skies in his majesty."[12]
- 1 Chronicles 16:27, "Splendor and majesty are before him; strength and joy in his place."
- 1 Chronicles 29:11, "Yours, O LORD, is the greatness and the power and the glory and the victory and the majesty, for all that is in heaven and earth is yours."

- Job 37:4, "He thunders with his majestic voice…"
- Job 37:22, "God is clothed with awesome majesty."
- Psalm 8:1, "O LORD, our Lord, how majestic is your name in all the earth!"
- Psalm 29:4, "The voice of the LORD is powerful; the voice of the LORD is full of majesty."
- Psalm 45:4, "In your majesty ride forth victoriously for the cause of truth and meekness, and righteousness; let your right hand teach you awesome deeds."
- Psalm 68:34, "Ascribe power to God, whose majesty is over Israel and whose power is in the skies."
- Psalm 93:1, "The LORD reigns; he is robed in majesty; the LORD is robed; he has put on strength as his belt."
- Psalm 96:6, "Splendor and majesty are before him; strength and glory are in his sanctuary."
- Psalm 104:1, "Bless the LORD, O my soul! O LORD my God, you are very great! You are clothed with splendor and majesty."
- Psalm 111:3, "Full of splendor and majesty is his work, and his righteousness endures forever."
- Psalm 145:5, "On the glorious splendor of your majesty, and on your wondrous works, I will meditate."
- Isaiah 24:14, "They lift up their voices, they sing for joy; over the majesty of the LORD they shout from the west."
- 2 Peter 1:17, "For when he received honor and glory from God the Father, and the voice was borne to him by the Majestic Glory, "This is my beloved Son, with whom I am well pleased."

What a list for proclaiming God's greatness! How can anyone read these verses and not praise Him? There's nothing and no one like our God, who is majestic and awesome.

Understanding God's majesty is significant for many reasons:

1. Only God is majestic; He is supremely great.
2. No other creature (angels, animals, humans) is majestic.

3. Worship is a natural response to God's majesty.
4. We approach God with awe, thankfulness, and humility.
5. God's majesty inspires us to live with faith, hope, love, and perseverance.

Although there are many reasons that affirm God's majesty, I have chosen to focus on the creation story. The creation story highlights God's majesty in light of His eternal nature and power.

Before the World Began (1:1)

Perhaps the most famous words in the Bible are the three first words of Genesis: "In the beginning…" Here and elsewhere, the Bible assumes and proclaims God's existence — and never attempts to prove it. God's eternal existence is a fact that's declared throughout the Scriptures (Genesis 21:33; Deuteronomy 33:27; Isaiah 26:4; Jeremiah 10:10; Habakkuk 1:12; Romans 16:23; 1 Timothy 1:17).

"From everlasting to everlasting," God is to be praised (1 Chronicles 16:36; Nehemiah 9:5; Psalm 41:13; 90:2; 106:48). God is eternal and everlasting; He was, is, and always will be. According to Genesis 1:1, God is the supreme king, ruler, and Lord of the universe and our world.

God's eternal nature also depicts who He is. The Bible uses the words "eternal," "everlasting," "everlasting to everlasting," and "forevermore" to highlight God's character and how He relates to us in several ways:

- Love (Psalm 103:17; Jeremiah 31:3)
- Name (Isaiah 56:5; 63:12)
- Pleasures (Psalm 16:11)
- Praise (Psalm 111:10)
- Kingdom (Psalm 145:13; Daniel 4:3; 7:27; 2 Peter 1:11)
- Dominion (Daniel 4:34; 7:14; 1 Timothy 6:16)
- Ways (Habakkuk 3:6)
- Power (Romans 1:20)
- Glory (2 Corinthians 4:17; 2 Timothy 2:10; 1 Peter 5:10)
- Purpose (Ephesians 3:11)

- Comfort (2 Thessalonians 2:16)
- Redemption (Hebrews 9:12)
- Covenant (Genesis 9:16; 17:7, 13, 19; 2 Samuel 23:5; 1 Chronicles 16:17; Psalm 105:10; Isaiah 24:5; 55:3; 61:8; Jeremiah 32:40; 50:5; Ezekiel 16:60; 37:26; Hebrews 13:20)
- Righteousness (Psalm 119:142; Daniel 9:24)
- Joy (Isaiah 61:7)
- Light (Isaiah 60:19–20)

What an amazing description of God's eternal character! God is truly majestic. When I consider God's eternal nature, two questions come to mind:

Is our God as big *as the Scriptures proclaim?*
Do we need to expand our thoughts?

What a Wonderful World (1:2–1:25)

Are you familiar with Louis Armstrong's song "What a Wonderful World"? Here are a few lines:

I see trees of green, red roses too.
I see them bloom for me and you.
And I think to myself, What a wonderful world.

I see skies of blue and clouds of white,
The bright blessed day, the dark sacred night,
And I think to myself, What a wonderful world.

Armstrong celebrates the beauty of the world. Look around. See the trees? See the skies? What about the oceans and mountains? What do you see? What do you hear? What a wonderful world!

Not only is God eternal, but He is all-powerful as well. God's awesome power is displayed in the creation story of Genesis. While

Christians have discussed different ways of interpreting the creation "days,"[13] everyone agrees on the most important point — God is the creator.

The stories in *Go Deeper* encourage us to place ourselves into the narrative, to think, feel, and experience. This is more challenging, however, with Genesis 1 because there's no literary character development. So, what should we do?

Here are two suggestions:

1. Read Genesis 1 as if you were in an IMAX theatre. As you read about God creating the light, sky, water, land, vegetation, sun, moon, stars, birds, fishes, and land animals, visualize them appearing on a huge IMAX screen while you are sitting in your movie seat.

2. Go to a mountain, lake, hiking trail, zoo, beach, park, or just sit outside in your backyard. As you read Genesis 1, thank God for His creation. Praise Him for His greatness![14]

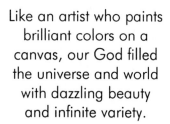

Like an artist who paints brilliant colors on a canvas, our God filled the universe and world with dazzling beauty and infinite variety.

Like an artist who paints brilliant colors on a canvas, our God filled the universe and world with dazzling beauty and infinite variety. All of this — from snowcapped mountains to farmlands, from the outer reaches of the universe to the deep depths of the seas, from the largest animals to the microscopic ones — God created everything from nothing. What a wonderful world!

God's creation is also called "good" (Genesis 1:4, 10, 12, 18, 21, 31). This is a magnificent statement! When we say creation is good, we are declaring that it reflects God's power. In addition, creation is called good because it has order and operates according its natural, physical laws (which God created and sustains). Also, a good creation refers to God's gifts to us for our enjoyment and His glory.

God's omnipotence (He is all-powerful) is not limited to the creation narrative, however. Scripture highlights several examples. As you read them, place yourselves in the shoes (or sandals) of those who experienced God's power:

- You witnessed the ten plagues (Exodus 7:14–11:10).
- You crossed the Red Sea (Exodus 13:17–14:29; 15:1–21).
- Elijah raised your dead son (1 Kings 17:7–24).
- You saw fire come down from heaven (1 Kings 18:16–40).
- Elisha had you taste "whole" water that was previously bitter (2 Kings 2:19–22).
- You (or your virgin wife) just gave birth to a child (Luke 1:26–56; 2:1–20).
- Jesus feeds you — one of 5,000 people (Mark 6:30–44).
- Jesus calms a heavy storm — you were in the boat (Luke 8:22–25).
- You are blind; Jesus heals you (John 9:1–41).
- You are a witness to Jesus's resurrection (1 Corinthians 15).
- The Holy Spirit comes; He sounds like a howling wind (Acts 2:1–4).
- You are crippled; Peter heals you (Acts 3:1–26).
- You are filled and empowered by the Spirit (Ephesians 5:18).

These are all examples of God's amazing power. Read this list again, but slowly.

What kind of thoughts and feelings do you have?

These biblical truths teach us three things about God's power. First, God's power testifies to His greatness. Because only God is omnipotent, He alone is majestic. Second, God's power teaches us about His character. God doesn't do miracles just for the sake of doing miracles. Rather, God's miracles reveal His heart of compassion, justice, mercy, and peace. Third, God's power confirms and authenticates that His message is true.

A Good Partnership (1:26–31)

So, what have we learned so far? First, God is majestic; He is eternal and all-powerful. Second, God's majestic creation reflects His awesome glory and power (Psalm 19:1–6). The third element of the Genesis 1 story is our majestic relationship with God. God created birds, fishes, and land animals, but only human beings have been created in God's image. Our partnership with God consists of three truths.

First, human beings were created in God's image. Being created in God's image is one of the most important truths. Let me share five observations (1) From a substance or nature view, we may say that we are like God because He created us with an intellect, emotions, and will. (2) We were created with a spiritual dimension. Because human beings have a soul/spirit, we have a desire for spiritual intimacy with God. (3) We are like God in our ability to create and we intrinsically desire things such as truth, justice, goodness, peace, love, joy, and beauty. We naturally reflect these kinds of characteristics because we are created like God.

(4) From a functional standpoint we are like God in being stewards of creation (birds, fish, crawling creatures, and environment). Thus, we enjoy leading, organizing, managing, healing, and restoring organizations and living organisms because these traits have been naturally created within us. (5) A person's biological life-span, physical, psychological, economic, social, or immoral behavior cannot erase the image of God (though the effects of sin have defaced God's image in us so that we are do not reflect God's image perfectly).

Second, human beings were created "good." (Genesis 1:31) But what does it mean to be "good?" (1) Adam and Eve did not originally possess any genetic flaws. They weren't born with any birth defects. There was no cancer or inability to see, hear, taste, touch, or smell. (2) They didn't have the psychological baggage that we have experienced in our broken families and social relationships.

(3) Adam and Eve had an intimate and dynamic relationship with God. Because sin had not entered into their relationship with God, they lived in and experienced perfect harmony with God. Adam and Eve were spiritually connected to God. A majestic God has created us in His image. Adam and Eve were created physically, psychologically, and spiritually "good." We have been created to find *ultimate satisfaction* with Him. A great God is seeking to have a relationship with us.

Third, God commands Adam and Eve to "be fruitful," "subdue" the earth, and "rule" over creation. In what has been referred to as "the cultural mandate" or "the creation mandate," God has called us to serve others to bring His glory to the world. How do we do this? We proclaim and bring God's truth to all forms of cultural activities such as (1) science, (2) law, (3) environmental studies, (4) art, (5) education, (6) literature, (7) media, (8) philosophy, (9) technology, (10) politics, and (11) economics.

This call of partnering with God does not mean that we create our own Christian culture. Rather, we impact and influence our world in light of our vocations. All vocations are divine callings of God. No vocation is greater or higher than another.[15] As we faithfully fulfill God's calling in our life, we proclaim the gospel and serve others with acts of justice and compassion. In short, being created in God's image is an amazing blessing, but this truth also challenges us to partner with God in light of serving our neighborhood, city, and world.

> As we faithfully fulfill God's calling in our life, we proclaim the gospel and serve others with acts of justice and compassion.

SUMMARY

1. When we say, "God is majestic," we are declaring that He is supremely great.
2. As the majestic creator, God is eternal. Everything and everyone owes their existence to God.
3. God's majestic creation reflects His awesome glory and power. God's power is demonstrated in His creating the world out of nothing, performing miracles, and empowering His people.
4. Our majestic relationship with God is based on being created by Him in His image. Human beings were originally created physically, psychologically, and spiritually "good."
5. God has also called us to partner with Him to bring His glory to the world through cultural activities (cultural mandate).

6. As the creator of the universe, God pursues us. He seeks to have an intimate and passionate relationship with us.

REFLECTION

1. Take time this week to be alone with God in nature. As you sit, walk, hike, or bike, consider God's greatness. Share your experience with someone at your church or in your small group.
2. Read about God's majesty again (background section). How does God's greatness lead you to worship Him?
3. How does God's power encourage you to trust Him?
4. What does Genesis 1:26–27 teach about the dignity of human beings created in God's image? What are the implications of this truth?
5. How are you fulfilling the cultural mandate? How can the cultural mandate lead to opportunities to share the gospel?
6. How has God, as the creator of the universe, been pursuing you? How is He pursuing your family and friends?

PRAYER FOR SPIRITUAL FORMATION

Dear Father,

You created the world. I praise you! Creation shows your power and mighty hand. All the stars, mountains, trees, lakes, and animals proclaim your glory. God, I worship you because you are great. Thank you for creating me in your image. I need your strength to fulfill my calling in life. Give me boldness to proclaim the gospel to my family and friends.

CHAPTER 3

ADAM AND EVE
Genesis 3:1–24

God's Judgment

Introduction

One afternoon my family (Peggy, William, Timothy) and I were sitting at a Korean all-you-can-eat buffet. The pork, chicken, and beef were being cooked — sizzling sounds and that distinct aroma began to pervade our booth. This was as good a time as any to talk about God's judgment.

"What stories in the Bible deal with God's judgment?" I asked.

Stories came pouring in such as Noah and the flood, Sodom and Gomorrah, the ten plagues against Egypt, Assyria and the northern kingdom, and Babylon and the southern kingdom.

"Good examples, but what about the New Testament?" A bit of a slowdown occurred. I think we just hit one of those famous Los Angeles traffic jams.

"Well, it just seems like God is more wrathful in the Old Testament," someone noted. This seemed to satisfy the group. I told everyone that we could eat while discussing this topic (for which they were thankful).

I mentioned Ananias and Sapphira (Acts 5:1–11), Herod (Acts 12:23), those taking communion in an unworthy manner (1 Corinthians 11:26–29), the seven churches in Revelation 2–3, and God's final judgment (Revelation 20:11–15) as examples of God's judgment in the New Testament. The most significant act of judgment in the New Testament is Jesus's death on the cross. Jesus became a sin offering for His people so that we could be forgiven for our sins, reconciled to God, and declared righteous (Romans 3:21-31; 2 Corinthians 5:21; Hebrews 10:1-18).

Background

The idea of God's judgment is related to His justice. On the one hand, God's justice refers to His response to evil and wickedness. "Justice," according to Augustine, "is that virtue which gives everyone his due." This expression of God's character is known as His retributive justice. In brief, justice is giving everyone what they deserve. Later, in chapter 5, I will discuss another aspect of God's justice: God's acts of mercy for the needy.

God's judgment is based on His ultimate standard of righteousness. When we say "God is just," we are saying that His judgments are right, fair, and deserving. Although God's judgment is not the most popular kind of sermon series, it's nevertheless, very important. Let me share a few thoughts on this idea.

First, although we may not like to talk about it, God's judgment occurs throughout the Scriptures. You can't get around it. The pages of our Bibles are filled with examples of God's judgment. Our God is a God of judgment. God's ultimate judgment assigns the wicked to hell (Revelation 20:7-15) and the righteous to the new heavens and the new earth (Revelation 21:1-22:5). But why is He like this?

Second, God's judgment is related to His holiness, righteousness, and our sin. Because He is holy, He is the ultimate standard of moral goodness and purity. Because God is righteous, we know that He will judge everyone impartially and justly. But why can't He be more like Jesus, who seems to talk more about love, grace, and mercy?

Third, although Jesus was full of grace and mercy, it is also significant to note that He talks about judgment and uses images associated with judgment more than any person in the Bible. How does He do this? Here are a few examples:

- People not entering God's kingdom (Matthew 5:20; 18:3–4)
- Judgment (Matthew 5:21, 5:22, 12:36–37; Matthew 10:15–11:24/Luke 10:1–15; Matthew 12:36; 12:41; 12:42; John 5:22; 5:30; 9:39)
- Fire (Matthew 13:31–43)
- Punishment (Matthew 25:31–46; Luke 16:19–31)
- Hell (Matthew 5:22, 29; Mark 9:47, 30; Mark 9:43, Matthew 10:28; 18:9; 23:15; 23:33; Luke 12:5; 16:23)

So what does all this mean? God's judgment is important for several reasons, in what His judgment reveals about creation and God Himself:

1. God is righteous and fair.
2. The universe has a moral law.
3. Our desire for fairness will be satisfied.
4. Sin has consequences.
5. Sharing the gospel should be a high priority.

Judgment Preceded by Sin (3:1–7)

Satan has a strategy for tempting us to sin. From this passage, we can learn three lessons. First, Satan masquerades sin and dresses it up so that it looks like everything else. Sin camouflages itself as good things

"Nice. Perfect. In the Garden of Eden, I see the man and woman. Since they are surrounded by all these animals, they won't be alarmed if I take on the form of one of them. I'll be a serpent and talk to the woman first."

Second, Satan wants us to doubt God's Word. Satan inquired of Eve, "Did God actually say, 'You shall not eat of any tree in the garden'?" (3:1).

Eve informs Satan that she will die if she eats from or touches the tree of the knowledge of good and evil, then Satan continues his deception: "You will not surely die" (3:4).

Satan tells Eve that "God knows that when you eat of it your eyes will be opened, and you will be like God, knowing good and evil" (3:5). In other words, God is keeping something from you. What kind of God is He if He keeps your eyes closed from experiencing what life has to offer?

Sin isn't too bad, is it?

Third, Satan makes the temptation unbearable if we fail to do something about it. Sometime later, Eve was alone with Adam. The temptation, however, had already been planted in her heart. How would she deal with it? Perhaps, she had already discussed this with Adam. We're not sure. If we do not flee from sin, meditate on God's Word, pray for strength, and/or find immediate support from another Christ-follower, then the temptation might be too strong to overcome.

What happened to Adam and Eve? The temptation became too strong. They acted on their desires. Both of them ate from the tree. It was a direct action against God's command.

Sin has now entered the world.

While it's true that Satan had had already rebelled against God, Adam and Eve's sin is the first time that sinned entered the relationship between God and human beings. Romans 5:11–21 teaches that Adam's sin has been transmitted to all human beings so that everyone is born a sinner (Psalm 51:5). We are not sinners because we sin. Rather, we sin because we are sinners.

> God's judgment, however, is His righteous response to sin.

Because God is holy, He must now act. His judgment must commence. Before we move forward with our discussion in *Go Deeper*, however, we need to remember that God's judgment was preceded by Adam and Eve's sin. If they don't sin, there's no judgment. If we don't sin, there's no judgment. God's judgment, however, is His righteous response to sin.

Hiding from God (3:8–13)

Adam and Eve heard the Lord as He was walking in the garden. Sometimes the Bible depicts God in human-like characteristics to help us understand Him. This literary device is called anthropomorphism. The author of Genesis also uses anthropomorphism to draw readers into the narrative. The purpose is to heighten interest and curiosity.

They hid from Him among the trees. God called to Adam, "Where are you?" (3:9). When we sin, we don't want God to find us. Perhaps, it's the guilt we're feeling. Some of us deny our sin. Adam and Eve attempted to hide.

Why do we hide from God?

Adam replied, "I heard the sound of you in the garden, and I was afraid, because I was naked, and I hid myself" (3:10). While it's true that Adam and Eve were both physically naked, their nakedness also symbolized their lost innocence and vulnerability before God. Sin exposes us before God.

As a result of their disobedience, they were also feeling a sense of shame. Adam and Eve became conscious of committing something improper and dishonoring to God. Their sin created a new painful emotion that they never experienced before. If left untreated, shame can also lead to other consequences such as inferiority, habitually destructive behavior, self-pity, passivity, isolation and withdrawal, loss of creativity, codependent relationships, and despising our appearance.[16]

Have you felt shame before?

Even though Adam and Eve try to hide from God, He continues to pursue them. God was giving them the opportunity to confess their disobedience. He wanted them to deal with their shame. "Who told you that you were naked? Have you eaten of the tree of which I commanded you not to eat?" (3:11). It's not that God was unaware of their sin. So what is God doing by asking such a question?

In response to their sin, God is pursuing Adam and Eve.

How did Adam react? "The woman whom you gave to be with me, she gave me fruit of the tree, and I ate." (3:12). Nice one, Adam. Blame it on Eve! It's all her fault! Perhaps, even more alarming is that behind Adam's blame game is really an attack on God's provision. "The woman you put here with me..." You placed Eve in Eden — it wasn't my choice. What a provocative statement!

God could have scolded Adam for his lack of responsibility and sin. But, He decides to continue the conversation. He wants to tease out the truth. He wants them to realize that they are responsible for their choices and actions. God asks Eve, "What is this that you have done?" (3:13).

Adam was given a chance to acknowledge his sin. He didn't. Maybe Eve will confess? Not a chance! "The serpent deceived me, and I ate" (3:13). Like Adam, Eve fails to take responsibility for her decision. In short, we have two guilty people hiding from God, who is pursuing them.

What are the common ways we hide from God?

How do you deal with shame?

Devastation and Brokenness (3:14–19)

Just like good parents who need to discipline their children, God is not the kind of Father who allows us to get away with disobedience. God's justice will bring judgment. Faustina Kowalska observed, "His justice is so great and penetrating that it reaches into the heart of things, and all things stand before Him in naked truth, and nothing can withstand Him."[17]

God hands out three judgments; one for Satan, one for Eve, and one for Adam. The serpent will now crawl on its belly for the rest of its life (3:14). More importantly, there will be a constant struggle between Satan and God's people. From this day forward, Satan, the adversary of God's people, will seek to tempt and spiritually attack Christ-followers (Ephesians 6:11-18). God proclaims to Satan that he "shall bruise his heel," but one of His people "shall bruise your head" (3:15).

Genesis 3:15 is the first example of the gospel, the good news. A future person (the Messiah), later revealed as a king, will bring justice, mercy, and peace. As the Divine King, Jesus is the fulfillment of this prophecy and has defeated Satan by dying on the cross and resurrecting from the dead (Romans 5:8; 2 Corinthians 5:21).

For Eve (and future women), the pains of childbirth and their vulnerability before men would greatly increase (3:16). It's not just the childbirth itself but, perhaps, the whole process of raising and disciplining faithful children in our world that is in sight here. Likewise, history testifies to how men have humiliated, overpowered, and treated women as objects of desire and possession.

For Adam (and future men), work would now be harder because the ground has been cursed. Whereas previously, before the fall, it would freely and easily produce fruit from labor, the intensity and hardship of that labor would now increase. Like humanity, creation needs to be restored (Romans 8:18–21). This curse on creation has affected men and women who seek to find their identity in work (3:17–18).

Next, God's devastating judgment brings death: "you are dust, and to dust you shall return" (3:19). Death means separation. *Physical* death is the separation of the soul/spirit from the body. But the consequences of sin go beyond physical death. Genesis 3 also refers to *spiritual* death. Spiritual death is separation from God (Romans 6:23). Our sin creates an infinite chasm between God and us.

Our brokenness affects our whole being, body and soul (Romans 3:9–20). Sin has also affected our relationships with one another. Here are several examples. (1) We experience a loss of dignity and respect for ourselves and toward one another. (2) We distrust and are suspicious of one another. (3) Love becomes more self-absorbing and manipulative. (4) We mask our lives through deception and fictional living. (5) There's a general spirit of competition and conflict between human beings.

In summary, sin has brought devastating consequences. Reconciliation must take place. We need to be reconciled to God. People, communities, and nations must also be reconciled to one another. Creation must also be restored.

Judgment Can Lead to Hope (3:20–24)

In the midst of judgment, the narrator of Genesis highlights Eve's significance (again) in 3:21, "Adam named his wife Eve, because she would become the mother of all the living." While it's true that sin brought death, Eve would bring life literally (birth of children) and spiritually (a future descendant would defeat Satan).

We are then informed that "the LORD God made garments of skin for Adam and his wife and clothed them" (3:22). Although we have no written record of what happened before 3:22, perhaps something like the following was said. "Your nakedness represents your sin. In order to cover your nakedness, you shall kill this animal. The animal's life will be a substitute for your lives to pay for your sin. Wear the animal skins as garments to remind yourself of your sin and my provision for you." These animal skins foreshadow the Old Testament sacrifices and ultimately find their fulfillment in Jesus's death on the cross as a substitute for our sins.

Then, Adam and Eve are shown the door. Get out of my garden! Some believe that God was being merciful when He kicked them out of Eden. [They] "must not be allowed to reach out [their] hand[s] and take also from the tree of life and eat, and live forever" (3:23). This banishment is so important that God takes extra precautions: He guards the entrance of Eden with a cherubim (a type of angel) and tree of life with a flaming sword (3:24).

> Forcibly removed from Eden, Adam and Eve began a new life and new adventure.

Forcibly removed from Eden, Adam and Eve began a new life and new adventure. This act of judgment, however, was also an opportunity for a new beginning with God, with one another, and with their created world. From the perspective of judgment and sin, Genesis 3 sounds pretty horrific, doesn't it? On the other hand, we can also look at it from another angle. How so?

Here are three ways that God's judgment can lead to hope:

1. God's judgment provides an opportunity for forgiveness.
   Are you tired of hiding from God? Has your guilty conscience caught up with you? What should you do? Confess your sins to God and ask for forgiveness. 1 John 1:9 states: "If we confess our sins, he is faithful and just to forgive us our sins and to cleanse us from all unrighteousness."

2. God's judgment provides an opportunity for repentance.
   Perhaps, you've realized that you've been traveling on a ship going the wrong way? What should you do? Turn the ship around! Jesus said, "I have not come to call the righteous but sinners to repentance" (Luke 5:32). Repentance is more than feeling sorry about something. Rather, it's coming to God with a broken spirit and making a willful choice to reject sin and seek God.

3. God's judgment provides an opportunity for a new beginning.
   Whenever I talk about spiritual formation, I always tell people that "it's never too late to plant a tree." Our God of judgment is also a God of new beginnings! 2 Corinthians 5:17 proclaims that "if anyone is in Christ, he is a new creation. The old has passed away; behold, the new has come."

God's judgment brought forth major consequences. His judgment, however, provides opportunity for hope. All three elements of hope — forgiveness, repentance, and a new beginning — were given to Adam and Eve. *These same opportunities for hope have also been given to us.*

SUMMARY

1. The Bible teaches that God is a holy and righteous judge. God's judgment is His response to our sins.

2. God's judgment brought devastating consequences:
   - Our sin has separated us from God and each other.
   - We need to be reconciled to God and each other.
   - Creation must be renewed.
   - Spiritual warfare between Satan and God's people
   - Women: childbirth, raising children, and exploitation
   - Men: work harder, identity found in work, and career

3. Like Adam and Eve, we try to hide from God. We experience shame.

4. As a judge, God is and has been pursuing us.

5. God's judgment of sin has been poured out on Jesus, who died as our substitute for our sin.

6. God's judgment can lead to hope:
   - The promise of the Messiah
   - Forgiveness
   - Repentance
   - New beginning

REFLECTION

1. The idea of God's judgment is a biblical one. Did you learn anything new about God's judgment? Explain.

2. Why do you think some people ignore or deny the idea of God judging us for our sins?

3. Does God's judgment take away from or contradict His love and mercy?

4. Have you experienced shame before? How do you hide from God? Share your answers with one of your Christian friends.

5. How can Jesus's death deal with your shame and encourage you to respond to God with gratitude and thanksgiving?

6. As a judge, God has been pursuing you. How can God's judgment provide hope for you?

7. How is God pursuing your unchurched family members, friends, and neighbors?

PRAYER FOR SPIRITUAL FORMATION

Dear Father,

I sin. I disobey you. You are a righteous judge. Help me to experience the Spirit's conviction. Like Adam and Eve, sometimes I want to hide and run from you. Jesus, thank you for taking away my sin and shame. God, help me to experience your love and forgiveness. My hope is in you alone. I need your wisdom to share the gospel with my family, friends, and neighbors.

CHAPTER 4

JOSEPH
Genesis 37–50

God's Sovereignty

Introduction

When I was growing up, I never thought about who I would marry. From my dad's side of the family, I am a third generation ABC (American-born Chinese) and from my mom's side, I'm a second generation ABC. If you're doing the math, that means I'm 2.5. Keep the calculator handy because I have more numbers to crunch!

Needless to say, my brothers and I are Americans from top to bottom in language, culture, and style. We didn't hear too much Chinese at home — the only time was when my parents were talking about money or we were eating Chinese food.

I was happy living in America and hanging out with Americans. I remember feeling "cool" when my friends referred to me as someone who wasn't like them ("them" meaning people who spoke Chinese aloud).

All this changed, however, when I started attending a Chinese church. My world was altered a bit. I was definitely being fed some new sound bites. Later, I attended a state college (where I eventually was dismissed on academic probation, but that's another story) and began dating a young woman from, of all places, Hong Kong!

As our relationship progressed, we became engaged. Peggy's father wanted me to get a taste of the Chinese culture so he encouraged me to apply for an English teaching job in Hong Kong. In order to satisfy him, I applied to only one school. What happened? This school accepted my application and offered me the job. So there I was, living in Hong Kong. I was surrounded by people who spoke Cantonese (much harder than Mandarin, but it doesn't matter if you don't know either).

A year later, I was married to a girl from Hong Kong! My two sons were also born in Hong Kong! I was a 2.5 gen living in Hong Kong. Are you ready for my math question? If I am 2.5 gen, then what are our sons? Okay, I probably lost you. They are 1.25 gen (unfortunately, Peggy receives a zero score for coming to America during her high school years).

> God has a plan that is way beyond what we think can or can't happen or should or shouldn't happen.

The upshot of all this is simple: God is sovereign. God has a plan that is way beyond what we think can or can't happen or should or shouldn't happen. God is in control. Even though I had no desire to be more Chinese, from a cultural standpoint, God's hand was working behind the scenes to make this all come about.

Background

Joseph is one of the most interesting characters in the Bible. When you read the narrative about his life, Joseph comes across pretty clean. Sure, he seems to hurt his brothers with his "I had a dream" speeches, but these dreams (for Joseph and not necessarily for us) were inspired by God (37:5-11). Also, he seems to have a little fun with his brothers by not revealing his true identity and placing the silver cup into Benjamin's bag (44:1-34).

(Some commentators explain this as Joseph's way of getting his brothers to experience guilt for their actions.)

Joseph goes through a lot. His brothers reject him because his father favored him and gave him an amazing coat (37:1-4). Is this Joseph's fault? I guess he could have said, "No thanks," but would you have rejected your father's gift? Joseph was also sold to people traveling in a caravan heading to Egypt and pronounced dead to his father (37:12-36). With brothers like this, who needs enemies?

But, through it all, God is with Joseph. Joseph finds favor while working for Potiphar (39:1-6) and he finds favor while in prison (for a crime he didn't commit) (40:1-23). He even finds favor from the Pharaoh and lands a job as his right-hand man (41:1-57).

Does all of this happen because this man can interpret dreams? Not really. All of this happened according to God's sovereign plan. Joseph receives favor from these people in authority because God's grace (unmerited favor) and sovereign plan were being played out in Joseph's life.

Benjamin Franklin noted, "I have lived a long time, sir, and the longer I live the more convincing proofs I see of this truth — that God governs in the affairs of men."[18] Joseph also could testify to this. He embraces the truth that God causes all things to work together for His good (Romans 8:28). Scripture teaches that God has a plan for His people and is in control of all circumstances. Here are several examples:

- God's promise to Abraham was fulfilled when the Israelites under Joshua's leadership settled in Canaan.
- Moses was a shepherd in Midian, then became a shepherd for the Israelites.
- Ruth, a Moabite widow, pledged her undying love to Naomi, her mother-in-law; she eventually married Boaz and became part of the Messianic line of Jesus.
- Esther was chosen as queen; then she's in a position of authority to intervene for her people.

- The book of Daniel highlights God's control over the kingdoms of the world.
- Saul was a persecutor of God's people, but was transformed into "Paul"; he became "the Apostle to the Gentiles."

From these examples, we learn that God's sovereignty is significant for many reasons:

1. God has a plan; He has a purpose for history.
2. Even though chaos seems to reign, God is in control.
3. Satan, evil people, or fate are not in control.
4. We deepen our trust in God and experience peace as we embrace His sovereign plan.

Horatio Spafford understood what it meant to place his life in the hands of a sovereign God. First, Spafford lost his real estate investments due to the Chicago Fire of 1871. Second, about two years later, he lost all four of his daughters to a sea tragedy, when the ship they were traveling aboard was struck by an English vessel (his wife survived). Spafford's "It is Well with My Soul" (first verse) draws from his experience of loss, pain, and God's sovereignty:

> When peace, like a river, attendeth my way,
> When sorrows like sea billows roll,
> Whatever my lot, Thou hast taught me to say,
> It is well, it is well with my soul.

Spafford experienced God's sovereignty and peace in the midst of his heartache. God's sovereignty also plays an important role in Joseph's life. Jacob, Joseph's father, had twelve sons from marriages (Leah, Rachel) and relationships (Bilhad, Zilpah). Jacob loved Rachel the most, however. Joseph was the first son born to Jacob and Rachel (eleventh son overall). As a result, Joseph was his father's favorite son.

Sibling Rivalry (37:1–36)

"He thinks he's so good."

"I can't believe he ratted on us," stammered another.

From a distance they could tell it was him.

"Yeah, that's him all right. I can't believe dad got him that robe. It must have cost a fortune."

How would you feel if one of your parents only gave your brother or sister an expensive gift?

This brings us to the first truth about God's sovereignty. God has the authority and privilege to do whatever He likes (though He won't do things that contradict His nature). When we say that God is sovereign, we are saying that He is in control. The Father giving the robe to Joseph is analogous to God choosing to bless and shower gifts on whomever He pleases.

The 17-year-old approached his brothers. "I have something interesting to share with you."

"What is it now?"

The teenager replied, "I wanted to share about some of my dreams."

"Who cares? Who wants to know," replied one of the brothers.

Another brother chimed in with sarcasm, "Wait, let the little guy share. I'm sure it will be entertaining."

The teenager spoke up: "Well, a week ago, I was dreaming that your stalks of grain bowed down to my stalks of grain."

This obviously didn't go well with his brothers. "So, we bowed down to you. You're so arrogant! Who do you think you are?"

A few days later, Joseph shared another dream with his brothers and later repeated it to his father and brothers:

"The sun, moon, and eleven stars were bowing down to me" (37:9).

In other words, different dream, same message: you're all going to kiss the ground that I walk on.

This only angered his brothers more. They couldn't wait to teach him a lesson.

Several days passed. Their anger and jealousy continued to escalate. Some even wanted to physically harm their brother. One day, the teenager was sent by his father to check on his brothers.

"Here comes the dreamer again."

"He's spying on us."

One of the brothers erupted, "Let's beat him."

Another brother did the first brother one better: "No, let's kill him."

Fortunately, the oldest brother Reuben had some grace:

"Are you serious? He's our own flesh and blood. Let's just dump him into this deep well here."

Eventually, his plan won out. (He said this in order to return later and rescue his father's favorite son.)

Grace saves life from death.

A few moments later, they caught their brother, stripped him of his fancy robe, threw him in the deep well, and began to eat their lunch.

Did you get that? After everything they did, they still managed to have a picnic!

Afterward, a caravan was coming toward them. They found out that it was headed toward Egypt. One of the brothers had an idea:

"Let's sell that punk brother of ours to these people. We can't kill him. After all, he is our brother." So, they sold their brother.

Later, Reuben returned to rescue Joseph. To his surprise, he was no longer in the deep well. The narrative does not provide us with any details about the whereabouts of Reuben when his brothers sold Joseph. It only informs us about his reaction to what had transpired. When Reuben learned what happened he knew that all the brothers would have to give an account to their father about his favorite son.

"We need a plan to explain all of this or we're all toast."

So the brothers schemed together. What was their story?

They found their brother's robe, dipped it in some animal blood. They would tell their father that Joseph had been ravaged by a wild animal.

"This looks good. I think our father will believe us."

"Now remember, we have to display our shock and grief to our father."

They approached their father with the look of horror on their faces. Some tore their clothes. Others were wailing. Tears were flowing down their faces. You've heard of drama queens before, right? Well, these men were drama kings!

Frantically, their father screamed: "What is it, my sons? What has happened?"

Upon hearing the news that his favorite son had been killed by an animal, the father broke down. He fell to his knees. He wept loudly and could not be comforted. "In mourning, I shall go to my son, to the place of the dead."

Unknown to them all, Joseph had been resold by those in charge of the caravan to Potiphar, the captain of the guard to Pharaoh.

For a Crime He Didn't Commit (39:1–23)

Have you lived in a foreign country before? I lived in Hong Kong for eight years. Although there were some exciting things about living in a foreign place, there were some major challenges too. Joseph was now a foreigner living in Egypt under the roof of a new master. Do you think God was punishing Joseph for something he did?

What kind of emotions do you think Joseph had? Anger? Was he screaming and seething? Perhaps he was plotting revenge? Not only was Joseph rejected by his brothers, but he was betrayed by them. To feel betrayed by one's loved ones is to experience something very powerful and hurtful. His own flesh and blood victimized Joseph. How would you feel if you were betrayed like Joseph?

Or, let's ask the bigger question of this story:

Where was God during this whole fiasco?

"The Lord was with Joseph, and he became a successful man" (39:2).

This leads us to our second lesson about God's sovereignty. Although God's sovereign will is infinitely beyond our comprehension and seems to make God distant and far away, just the opposite is true. God is intimately close to us. The sovereign God who made the heavens and the earth — His very presence was with Joseph.

> The sovereign God who made the heavens and the earth — His very presence was with Joseph.

And His presence is with you too.

In addition to finding favor in God's eyes, Joseph found favor with Potiphar as well. Potiphar observed how God was blessing Joseph's efforts in all his duties and responsibilities. So, Potiphar placed Joseph in charge of the household and everything that he owned.

Joseph goes from rags to riches. And the story doesn't end there.

Weeks now pass, perhaps several months. Joseph also caught the eye of Potiphar's wife. She begins to make advances toward him. Each time, however, Joseph rejects her. Do you find this part of the narrative too close for comfort? What's going on in Joseph's life?

"Joseph, no one needs to know. It will be our secret."

It's said that all that sin needs to be successful is opportunity. What do we do when we have the opportunity for sexual sin?

Sin is alluring.

Sin is attractive.

Sin traps us.

Sin takes hold of us.

What would you have done if you were Joseph?

Joseph flees. He knows that his flesh is weak. He takes off. Joseph runs away from sin.

In her attempt to deal with Joseph's rejection, Potiphar's wife brings a false accusation against him. She first informs the other servants and then Potiphar himself. "The Hebrew servant, whom you have brought among us, came in to me to laugh at me. But as soon as I lifted up my voice and cried, he left his garment beside me and fled out of the house" (39:17–18).

That's all Potiphar needs to hear. His wife has been attacked. Feeling betrayed and burning with anger, he placed Joseph in prison. As far as we know, there was no trial. No defense lawyer. Potiphar is judge and jury. But can you blame Potiphar?

Or, perhaps, should we blame God?

Most of us have heard of the phrase, "You do the crime, you do the time." We understand that when you break the law, there will be consequences. But what about doing the time for a crime you didn't commit?

That's what happened to Joseph — imprisoned for a crime he didn't commit. Have you ever wondered why Potiphar didn't get a sword to end Joseph's life? Why didn't he just rid himself of this disgusting Hebrew slave? The final verses of chapter 39 provide a clue to why Potiphar didn't take Joseph's life:

"But the LORD was with Joseph and showed him steadfast love and gave him favor in the sight of the keeper of the prison....The keeper of the prison paid no attention to anything that was in Joseph's charge, because the LORD was with him. And whatever he did, the LORD made it succeed" (39:20–23).

What's the answer for Potiphar's restraint?

The Lord was with Joseph.

But there's another issue that gnaws at our souls. "Why do bad things happen to good people?" While this question is beyond the scope of *Go Deeper*, John Piper provides a partial answer. "This is God's universal purpose for all Christian suffering — more contentment in God and less satisfaction with self."[19] Thus, God was sovereignly pursuing Joseph so that he would find satisfaction and contentment with Him.

> God was sovereignly pursuing Joseph so that he would find satisfaction and contentment with Him.

How are you finding spiritual satisfaction in the midst of God's sovereign plan?

Tell Me Your Dreams (40:1–41:57)

While Joseph was in prison the cupbearer and baker of the king of Egypt were sent to the same prison. Observing their downcast faces, Joseph inquired why they were so dejected. Besides being in prison (an obvious reason), they had dreams that needed to be interpreted.

Have you wondered why these men were so stressed about not having someone to interpret their dreams? The text doesn't explain, so we can only speculate. Was there someone in the palace who interpreted dreams? Or perhaps God caused these dreams to produce a deep anxiety? Maybe it was a combination of both.

Claiming that all interpretations belong to God, Joseph interprets both dreams. The first dream would have a happy ending while the second one would end with doom. The chief cupbearer would be restored to his place in three days and the chief baker would be hanged on a tree (birds would also come to devour his flesh). Both of these events happened just as Joseph said they would.

Joseph asked the chief cupbearer to put in a good word for him. "Only remember me, when it is well with you, and please do me the kindness to mention me to Pharaoh, and so get me out of this house. For I was indeed stolen out of the land of the Hebrews, and here also I have done nothing that they should put me into the pit" (40:14–15). The chief cupbearer, however, forgot about Joseph.

People may forget us. Friends may forget us. Family may forget us. God never forgets us, however. The author of Genesis wants to show the contrast between chapter 39 and 40. In chapter 40, the cupbearer forgets Joseph, but in chapter 39, the Lord was with Joseph. God never forgets Joseph. God knows Joseph.

And He knows you too.
You may be alone, but God has not forgotten you.
God has a plan for you.

A few years later, the cupbearer remembers Joseph's gift of interpreting dreams and the Pharaoh calls for Joseph. Being forgotten for those two years must have been discouraging. Have you ever felt like this? What were your circumstances? The pain we feel is real. What should we do? Give up? Lose hope? Do we dare to believe in a future?

Joseph had a proper understanding of God's sovereignty. Like the cupbearer and baker, the Pharaoh was greatly distressed. He needed someone to interpret a dream for him. Giving all the glory to God— "It is not in me; God will give Pharaoh a favorable answer," (41:16) Joseph tells the Pharaoh that he will have seven good years (good cows, good heads of grain) followed by seven years of famine (lean cows, worthless grain).

Joseph's attitude illustrates the third truth of God's sovereignty. The first truth is that He has all the authority and power to do what He pleases. The second truth is that God's with us—He's intimately close to us. receives all the praise and glory. Even though we may not understand God's sovereignty, His plan should lead us to worship and praise.

Recognizing that God was with Joseph, Pharaoh makes Joseph the leader of his palace with the responsibility of overseeing the land. Joseph is given the signet ring, fine robes, rides in a chariot, and serves as second-in-command of Egypt. God has blessed Joseph beyond his wildest imagination! Because God had revealed this plan to Joseph, the nation of Egypt became wealthy. Many countries had to come to Egypt for grain during the famine.

God has been pursuing Joseph with His sovereign plan.

God's Plan is Good (42–50)

One of the countries suffering from the famine was Canaan. Joseph's family lived in Canaan. Jacob sends all his sons (except Benjamin) to Egypt to get some grain. Because they have not seen Joseph for several years, his brothers could not recognize him. In fulfillment of Joseph's dream, his brothers unknowingly bow down to him. If God says something is going to happen, then it will. It may not occur when we want it to occur or think it should occur, but it will come to pass according to God's plan and His timetable.

The following chapters (43–47) describe Joseph's interaction with his brothers. His elaborate plan was to get their father (Jacob) and youngest brother (Benjamin) to come to Egypt. It was also a plan to cause his brothers to remember what they had done to Joseph. Chapters 48–49 record Jacob's arrival in Egypt and his blessing of Joseph's sons Manasseh and Ephraim as well as Jacob's own sons.

The final chapter (50) deals with the aftermath of Jacob's death. Joseph's brothers are worried that he will extract revenge on them for how they treated him. Not wishing to suffer the consequences for their actions, they plead with him, "Behold, we are your servants" (50:18). Joseph, however, shocks everyone. "As for you, you meant evil against me, but God meant it for good, to bring it about that many people should be kept alive, as they are today." (50:20).

This is the fourth and final truth of God's sovereignty. God's plan is working things out for the good (cf. Romans 8:28). It may not be what *we* think and feel is good, but according to God's infinite knowledge and wisdom, it's good. Can you imagine how the brothers must have felt after hearing Joseph proclaim God's sovereignty?

Perhaps, a better question is…

Can you imagine the kind of faith Joseph had as God continued to pursue him with His sovereign plan? This sovereign plan included Joseph being:

- Rejected by his brothers
- Sold to people traveling in a caravan going to Egypt
- Falsely accused by Potiphar's wife
- Imprisoned for a false crime
- Forgotten in prison

Although Joseph had times when he was sad, discouraged, and anxious about his life, his focus was not in trying to understand God's infinite plan. Rather, his faith was based on who God is — His character. Joni Eareckson Tada in *Is God Really in Control* observes, "Real satisfaction comes not in understanding God's motives, but in understanding His character, in trusting in His promises, and in leaning on Him and resting in Him as the Sovereign who knows what He is doing and does all things well."[20]

In short, God has a plan for us. To what extent do we embrace God's plan? How has God been pursuing you in the past years, months, or weeks? What has He been doing to grab your attention?

SUMMARY

1. Because God is sovereign, He has all the authority and power to do what He pleases. He won't, however, contradict His character.
2. God's sovereignty does not mean that He is far away. In fact, it means just the opposite — He is with us because it's His plan we are living.
3. In the midst of understanding God's sovereign plan for our lives, He should receive all the glory and praise.

4. God's sovereign plan works things out for good. It may not be according to our limited understanding of "good," but it's according to God's infinite knowledge and wisdom.

5. When we learn to trust and have faith in God's sovereignty, we are (eventually) liberated from thoughts and feelings of anger, bitterness, jealousy, and revenge.

REFLECTION

1. What is the most challenging part of submitting to God's sovereign plan?

2. Have you experienced betrayal before? To what extent have you been able to share about this experience? How should we deal with feelings of betrayal?

3. Joseph embraces God's plan for his life. Identify some practical ways for embracing God's sovereignty.

4. How has God been pursuing you in the past several weeks? What has He been doing to grab your attention?

5. How can trusting in God's sovereignty lead to worship, prayer, and serving others?

6. God has also been sovereignly pursuing your Christian brothers and sisters. How can this truth bring comfort and peace to them? Is there someone you need to encourage?

7. God has been sovereignly pursuing your family and friends. Explain how the truth of God's sovereignty helps you to begin spiritual conversations with them.

PRAYER FOR SPIRITUAL FORMATION

Dear God,

You are sovereign over the universe. When I experience trials, I want to do things my way. Sometimes, I get angry. I want to blame you. Father, help me to trust you even when I hurt. Give me strength to embrace your plan like Joseph. Because you are in control, I praise you. Help me to be a source of encouragement to my family and friends.

CHAPTER 5

MOSES
Exodus 3:1–21

God's Holiness

Introduction

In general, people have two reactions to fire. In one corner of the room, we have those who are captivated and excited by fire. When these people were younger they lived for camping. With their faces glowing, they would throw anything and everything into the pit. They love the blazes! They have a gift for roasting or, rather, setting marshmallows on fire as well. If they were anywhere near a fire pit or barbecue, they were the ones jumping, running, and screaming. These people were passionately drawn to the fire.

In the other corner of the room, we have those who don't want anything to do with fire. Guess which corner of the room I'm standing in? When I was younger, I wasn't too fond of the fire (I still ask Peggy for heavy oven gloves). I've roasted my share of hotdogs and marshmallows (perfectly light brown), but I really didn't enjoy getting up close and personal with those red-orange flames. I'm one of those people who keep their distance from the fire.

God's holiness is like fire. Some people are drawn closer to God because He is holy. These people realize that, first of all, only through Christ can they be forgiven and reconciled to a holy God. Because they understand that they are so far away from God's holiness, they have a passionate desire to draw near to Him. Like fire, God's holiness can purify.

> Like fire, God's holiness can purify.

At the same time, however, there are people who fear God and try to hide from Him (this is not the reverent kind of fear). Such people want to keep their distance from God because His holiness will reveal their shortcomings (the Bible calls these shortcomings "sin"). Like fire, God's holiness for these people is "too hot to handle."

Background

Our God is a holy God. This means first of all that He is radically different from His creation. Holiness in this sense means "set apart." Thus, something that is holy has been set apart and consecrated for God's glory and service. Second, holiness refers to God as the absolute and perfect standard of moral goodness and purity.

Before learning about Moses's holy encounter with God, we will highlight how Scripture uses the word "holy":

- God makes the seventh day holy (Genesis 2:3; Exodus 20:8).
- God's presence made the ground holy (Exodus 3:5; Joshua 5:15).
- God's dwelling is holy (Exodus 15:13).
- Israel was and is called to be a holy nation (Exodus 19:6; 22:31).
- Mount Sinai is holy (Exodus 19:23).
- In the tabernacle, there is a holy place and most holy place (Exodus 26:33).
- An altar can be most holy (Exodus 29:37).
- The tabernacle is holy (Exodus 40:9).
- The book of Leviticus is full of holiness!

- God is holy (Joshua 24:19; 1 Samuel 2:2; 6:20; Psalm 99:3, 5, 9; Revelation 15:4).
- God's name is holy (1 Chronicles 16:10; Psalm 30:4; 33:21; Isaiah 57:15; Ezekiel 20:39).
- God's temple is holy (1 Chronicles 29:3; Psalm 5:7; 11:4; 65:4).
- God's ways are holy (Psalm 77:13).
- God is holy, holy, holy (Isaiah 6:3; Revelation 4:8).
- God is the holy one of Israel (Isaiah 31:1; 37:23; 41:14, 16, 20).
- God's Spirit is Holy!
- God's covenant is holy (Luke 1:72).
- Jesus is holy (Acts 4:27, 30; 13:35; Hebrews 7:26).
- The Scriptures are holy (Romans 1:2; 2 Timothy 3:15).
- The law is holy (Romans 7:12).
- We offer our bodies as holy sacrifices (Romans 12:1).
- We are called to be holy (1 Corinthians 1:2; Ephesians 1:4; Colossians 1:2; 3:12; 1 Thessalonians 4:7; 2 Timothy 1:9; Titus 1:8; 1 Peter 1:15–16; 2 Peter 3:11; Revelation 22:11).
- We are made holy through washing of the word (Ephesians 5:26).
- We are declared holy in God's sight through Jesus Christ (Colossians 1:22; 1 Thessalonians 3:13).
- We need to control our bodies for holy living (1 Thessalonians 4:4).
- We become holy for God's purposes (2 Timothy 2:21).
- We are made holy through Jesus's sacrifice (Hebrews 10:10, 14; 13:12).
- Noah had holy fear (Hebrews 11:7).
- We can't see God without holiness (Hebrews 12:14).
- We are a holy priesthood (1 Peter 2:5).
- We are a holy nation (1 Peter 2:9).

What a great list! There's something awesome going on when we proclaim God's holiness. Moving from general to particular, the episode of Moses and the burning bush represents a story of God's holiness.

Moses lived 120 years. These years can be approximately divided into three sets of forty years: forty years in Egypt in the Pharaoh's palace, forty years as a shepherd in Midian, and forty years with the Israelites wandering in the wilderness. The book of Exodus, however, primarily focuses on the last forty years (Exodus 3–40). Moses is one of those bigger-than-life characters in the Bible.

Some of the most famous stories about Moses include being sent down the Nile as a baby, encountering God through a burning bush, directing the ten plagues, liberating the Israelites from Pharaoh, crossing the Red Sea, receiving the Ten Commandments and the Law, "seeing" the backside of God, receiving instruction for the tabernacle, and appearing with Elijah on the Mount of Transfiguration (in the New Testament).

Moses would be one of those people you would invite to a party because of the awesome stories he could tell you. "Hey, Moses, tell us another one." "Jim, there's Moses. Ask him to tell you about crossing the Red Sea. You're gonna go crazy." "Moses, how did it feel to receive the Ten Commandments?"

While all these stories are amazing, I believe Moses's encounter with God through the burning bush plays the most important role for the rest of his life and for the nation of Israel. I believe it's the most foundational because Moses experienced a holy God for the first time. This holy experience set him apart for God's service as well.

God's holiness is important for many reasons:

1. God is totally set apart from His creation; neither humans nor angels or anything or anyone can rival God's greatness.
2. God is the absolute standard of moral goodness and purity.
3. God's holiness reveals our sin and leads us to repentance.
4. Because we're sinners, we can never reach God's standard.
5. God's holiness does not outweigh His desire to have an intimate and passionate relationship with us through Jesus.
6. When God judges, He will judge with an ultimate moral standard.

Just Another Day (3:1–3)

"What am I doing here?"

"Before, I had it all…

a luxurious palace, servants at my beckoning call, the tastiest foods, and the finest drinks.

Now, I'm living in this dry and desolate place. Water is not easy to come by. I watch sheep. I count sheep. I feed sheep. I lead sheep. This isn't the way it was supposed to be."

What about you?

What are you doing here?

Where have you come from?

Where are you going?

"This looks like a good place to take a break. It's blazing hot." Something caught his attention. He began to move toward this plant or shrub. As the man gets closer, he notices something amazing.

What?

Are you serious?

A burning bush on a mountain?

The bush was on fire for God.

The fire symbolizes God's holiness.

What seemed like just another day turned into something life changing. God's holiness was going to transform this person's life. He would never be the same again.

What kind of person would you be if you were transformed by God's holiness?

Take Off Your Sandals (3:4–10)

A voice called out from the burning bush. "Moses! Moses!"

"I'm right here."

~~~~~~~~~~

Moses hides his face because God's holiness produced an overwhelming sense of awesome and reverent fear in him.

~~~~~~~~~~

"Do not come near; take your sandals off your feet, for the place on which you are standing is holy ground" (3:5).

God's holiness shatters us — from the inside out.

A voice continues to speak from the bush:

"I am the God of your father, the God of Abraham, the God of Isaac, and the God of Jacob" (3:6).

Without hesitation, Moses hides his face. But, why does he hide his face? In the words of Rudolph Otto's, *The Idea of the Holy*, Moses was experiencing the *mysterium tremendum* (awful mystery).[21] Moses hides his face because God's holiness produced an overwhelming sense of awesome and reverent fear in him. Never before in his eighty years of breathing did Moses experience this awful mystery (God) in this way.

Moses came to this realization...

he was a sinner in the presence of a holy God.

Have you ever experienced God's holiness in this way?

Moses's experience provided him with an opportunity for examining himself in light of God's holiness. What about us? Do we see ourselves in this manner? Like Moses, we are sinners in the presence of God's holiness. In light of this relationship, we need to ask ourselves some hard questions. Here's a list of questions to consider — a way to search our hearts before God:

1. Are you involved in any improper relationship?
2. How does pop culture influence your desire for holiness?
3. What do you allow your eyes to see and your ears to hear?
4. Which websites do you surf?
5. Would your private life cause embarrassment or shame?
6. To what extent do you treat your body as God's holy temple?
7. When was the last time you fell to your knees in an act of true repentance?
8. Is your heart so callous that questions such as these no longer stir you to consider holy living?

God's holiness, His divine presence also makes every day, common things — like the dirty ground — holy. God is in the business of making dirty things holy. He enjoys taking common things like broken people and transforming us into someone special, someone beautiful. To encounter a holy God would be an extraordinary experience. It would also lead to some thought-provoking questions as well.

Two Important Questions (3:11–15)

God was calling Moses to liberate the Israelites from Pharaoh. In response, Moses had two questions for God. Question 1: "Who am I?" In other words, Moses was struggling with his significance. He was feeling that he was not good enough to do the work that God was calling him to do.

Do you think or feel this way? But God, I'm just a...

Teacher
Single adult
Shy person
Engineer
Anxious person
Housewife
Teenager
Broken person
Mechanic
Grandparent
Part-time employee
Divorced husband or divorced wife
Lonely person

How does a holy God respond?
"I will be with you."
This truth is ultimately and completely revealed in Jesus, who is called "Immanuel," which means "God with us" (Isaiah 7:14).

"A true love of God," notes Jonathan Edwards, "must begin with a delight in his holiness."[22] This kind of holiness was designed to draw Moses into a deeper relationship with God. God tells Moses that He will walk with him during the most challenging and gut-wrenching times of his life.

What I find interesting here is God's purpose for liberation. "But I will be with you, and this shall be the sign for you, that I have sent you: when you have brought the people out of Egypt, you shall serve God on this mountain" (3:12). What does this mean? It means that we were created to worship God! John Piper says, "Missions is not the ultimate goal of the church. Worship is. Missions exist because worship doesn't."[23]

Question 2: "Who are You?" Moses can't just walk into the Pharaoh's palace and demand to let the Israelites go free. He's going to think Moses is crazy. The Pharaoh's going to ask who sent him with this obnoxious request. So God, who are you?

"I AM WHO I AM" (3:14). In Hebrew, the word is "Yahweh." Yahweh is God's sacred name, the name by which God wants to be known and remembered. Not only does Yahweh mean that God has always existed (in Hebrew it means something like "The Self-Existent One"), but it also highlights God's desire for establishing a relationship with His people. God wants something bigger, something better from us. He wants us to *Go Deeper*.

> God wants something bigger, something better from us. He wants us to **Go Deeper**.

These are two of the most important questions we can ask. Question 1 is for everyone: "Who am I?" Question 2 is for God: "Who are You?" How we answer the first question and respond God's answer to the second question will determine how we live on earth today and spend our lives for an eternity.

Marching Orders (3:16–22)

Moses encountered a holy God. Then God revealed Himself to Moses by informing him about His sacred name. Moses learned that God passionately seeks a relationship with us premised on holiness. This holy relationship would then lead to God's call to worship and serve Him. In order for us to do worship and serve God, however, we need to purify our hearts. Like metals that have been purified by fire, Christ-followers, must also choose to be holy.

What happens after God answers Moses's two questions? God gives Moses his marching orders. It's time to serve! Holiness leads to service! Gather the elders of Israel and tell them that He — the Lord is going to lead them out of bondage and into "a land flowing with milk and honey." What a description. Now that's what I call a word picture.

Then, God summarizes Moses's future encounter with Pharaoh. Moses, you're going to tell the Pharaoh this awesome plan of liberation, but he's not going to listen. He's a bit stubborn and selfish. But, that's okay because "I will stretch out my hand and strike Egypt with all the wonders that I will do in it; after that he will let you go" (Exodus 3:20).

This is how Exodus, chapter 3, ends: God informs Moses about His impending act of salvation. He will liberate His people from the chains of Pharaoh. Exodus chapter 3 ends where your life begins. As God's holiness continues to spiritually transform you, He also calls you to serve Him humbly, courageously, and faithfully.

SUMMARY

1. We define the idea of God's holiness in two ways:
   - To say that "God is holy" means that He is radically set apart from His creation due to His nature.
   - God is the absolute standard of moral goodness and purity.
2. God's holiness draws people into an intimate relationship with Him or it causes people to hide from Him.
3. God's holiness transforms common things for His glory and sets us apart (makes us holy) for serving other people.
4. Moses's encounter with God reveals two of the most important questions we can ask:
   - Of ourselves: Who am I to do God's work?
   - Of God: Who are You?
5. God gives everyone marching orders. He calls us to bring the message of salvation to our family members, friends, and neighbors. Salvation leads to worship and service.

REFLECTION

1. How would you feel if you were standing on holy ground like Moses? How would you react? What would you say to God?

2. God pursues us with His holiness. Does God's holiness draw you closer to Him or keep you at a distance from Him? Explain.

3. How can examining our hearts before a holy God make a difference in our lives? Find someone at your church or in your small group to share your thoughts.

4. How can understanding God's holiness play a role in developing your heart for worship?

5. The Apostle Paul refers to Christ-followers as "saints" because they have been set apart (made holy) for God's service. How is God asking you to serve Him?

6. Explain the relationship between living holy lives and spiritual accountability. Is there someone (besides your spouse) with whom you are accountable? Find someone as soon as possible!

7. How is God pursing your family and friends with His holiness? How does the idea of God's holiness create opportunities for you to share the gospel with them?

PRAYER FOR SPIRITUAL FORMATION

Dear Father,

You are a holy God. You are absolutely good and morally righteous. Like Moses, I'm a sinner in your holy presence. God, you call your people to live holy lives. Search my heart. Reveal my sins. With your Word, transform me from the inside out. Thank you for setting me apart to serve you. I ask for opportunities to deepen relationships with my family and friends.

CHAPTER 6

NAOMI
Ruth 1:1–22

God's Justice and Redemptive Community

Introduction

I wanted to address her question from a *different* perspective.

"Sara, I think you're right about the pain in the world and in your life. I would never deny or explain that away." She looked a bit indifferent. I paused for a few moments and then continued. "In response to the pain and suffering, what do you think about the idea of partnering with God?"

"Ken, isn't that the problem?" Now, with a touch of sarcasm: "God isn't powerful enough or doesn't love us enough to do something. Why does this great God need our help?"

I could have responded in several ways that focused on the philosophical nature of the question, but I chose *not* to reply to Sara with any of these points.[24] I could sense that her concern was primarily personal and experiential. I wanted to gently press my previous observation.

"Sara, human beings have also been given the responsibility and challenge to stamp out evil. God works in, with, and through us to defeat evil. May I explain?"

"Okay."

"We have used political means for ending slavery and bringing criminals to justice. Humanity has made tremendous scientific, medical, and technological advances for treating diseases and preventing new ones. We can also provide comfort for those who are suffering by building homes, providing food and clothing, and serving others with acts of compassion and justice."

I could tell that my answer didn't satisfy her. I did, however, give her reason to pause. I waited a few seconds. "Sara, I would like to share a few things this morning. Okay?"

"Sure. Go ahead."

"I would like to explain how a redemptive community serves people in need."

Another pause...I could tell by the look on her face that she was intrigued.

I continued. "Are you familiar with the story of Naomi?"

"Yeah...a little...I don't recall all the details."

I wanted to show Sara how she could place herself into the story of Naomi. "Sara, Naomi is a biblical character in the Old Testament. If you have a few minutes, I would like to share her story. I think you will be able to relate to Naomi in a personal and experiential way."

Background

One way to interpret the book of Ruth is to highlight the idea of a redemptive community. Ruth's spiritual community lived in Bethlehem. They worshiped the God of Abraham, Isaac, and Jacob. Ruth's community believed that God had revealed Himself by liberating their people from the Pharaoh and made a covenant with them through the prophet Moses.

In order to explain this theme, I will discuss the biblical concepts of redemption, justice, and community. Then, I will offer a brief definition of what it means to be a redemptive community. Regarding the notion of redemption, I will make two observations. First, redemption in the Old Testament refers to the deliverance of a person, property, or animal based upon the payment or price of a redeemer (Exodus 13:13; Numbers 18:15-16). In the New Testament, the primary meaning of redemption refers to Jesus redeeming us from our sins (Mark 10:45; Romans 3:24; 2 Corinthians 5:21; Ephesians 1:7).

Second, the majority of usages in the Old Testament refer to the physical deliverance of people from suffering and painful conditions. God hears the cries of the hurting and seeks to rescue the needy from their dire circumstances. The New Testament follows a similar pattern and exhorts us to redeem the whole person — body and soul. Redemption is not complete until the body and soul of a person reaches its glorified state.

I will also make two points about justice:[25] First, In addition to "acquitting or punishing every person on the merit of the case,"[26] justice may also refer to the proper and right relationships of people with one another. Justice carries the idea of establishing and upholding the rights of others. For this chapter, I will use this second definition of justice.

Second, God's character reveals what justice means. Psalm 146:7–9, for instance, proclaims that God "upholds the cause of the oppressed," "gives food to the hungry," "sets prisoners free,'" "gives sight to the blind," "lifts up those who are bowed down," "watches over the alien," and "sustains the fatherless and the widow" (cf. Deuteronomy 10:17–18).

Concerning the concept of community, I will share three thoughts. First, God Himself lives in a community of relationships: The Father, Son Jesus, and Holy Spirit demonstrate a relationship of love, unity, and submission (John 14:15–30; 15:26–16:15).

Second, God has created us in His image (Genesis 1:26–28). One aspect of being created in this manner is that we have been created to be in relationships with one another. Regardless of our ethnicity, social status, finances, careers, or marital status, we are called to live in unity (Galatians 3:26–28).

Third, because of our doubts and weaknesses, we need each other for mutual love, encouragement, accountability in light of God's Word, prayer, worship, and service (Ecclesiastes 4:9–12; Romans 14:19; 1 Corinthians 13; Colossians 2:1–15; Hebrews 4:12; James 5:13–19).

With this brief understanding of redemption, justice, and community we may define a redemptive community in the following way. A redemptive community is a group of people who (1) have been saved and reconciled to God, (2) meet together for spiritual growth, and (3) serve others with acts of compassion and justice. In brief, the idea of a redemptive community goes beyond the traditional understanding of a small group Bible study. The Scriptures call us to live a life of love, justice, and mercy

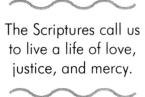

The Scriptures call us to live a life of love, justice, and mercy.

(Deuteronomy 10:17–18; 27:19; Job 29:12–17; Psalm 146:7–9; Proverbs 31:9; Micah 6:8; Zechariah 7:10–11; Luke 2:16–21; Acts 6:1–4; James 1:27; 1 John 3:16–20).

As we consider the importance of these key traits, we will begin to realize the significance of being part of a redemptive community. The relationship between God's justice and being a redemptive community is significant for a few reasons:

1. We can grow in our trust of God because we know that God's justice will ultimately reign.
2. We know that God is not indifferent to the cries of the needy.
3. We can partner with God to bring justice to our neighbors, society, and the world.
4. Our acts of compassion and justice are not ends in themselves (though they are good) because our objective is for people to be saved and to participate in community.

When Tragedy Strikes (1:1–5)

The relationship between God's justice and being a redemptive community plays a key role in the book of Ruth. Chapter 1 describes how God pursues Naomi until she chooses to return to her redemptive community.

Verse 1:1 provides the historical context for this story, "In the days when the judges ruled." This was one of the darkest times morally and spiritually in Israel's history because "the people of Israel did what was evil in the sight of the LORD" (Judges 2:11; 3:7; 3:12; 4:1; 6:1; 6:17; 10:6; 13:1). In the midst of this darkness, however, there are examples of redemptive communities that live faithfully.

One of the most important truths is that Christians do not walk around with bulletproof vests. Christians get cancer. Christians lose homes in fires, earthquakes, and tsunamis. Christians have psychological and emotional breakdowns. Christians have financial troubles.

God's people also experience famine and lose loved ones, too.

Because of a famine in the land of Judah, Elimelech and Naomi (with their two sons) departed from Bethlehem in Judah to Moab. The text does not explain the extent of the famine, but it was severe enough for them to leave their faith community. What is also interesting (and ironic from a literary standpoint) is that God's people were experiencing hunger in Bethlehem, a word that means "house of food."

While in Moab, tragedy strikes the family twice. First, Naomi's husband died. Being a widow during biblical times was especially difficult because the husband was responsible for physically sustaining the family. The emotional pain of dealing with the death of her spouse would have thrown Naomi into a grieving crisis. It would be normal for Naomi to experience some of these feelings:

Shock
Guilt
Depression
Anger
Loneliness
Distress
Restlessness
Emotional numbness[27]

In addition to these feelings, it wouldn't be surprising if Naomi also had questions about God's care for her family. Why did God allow this to happen? Where is God during my crisis? How will I live in this foreign country without my husband?

And just when you think Naomi's life can't get any worse something else happens...

Within ten years of her husband's death, a second tragedy strikes. Naomi's two sons die without having any children (they were married to Moabite women). Marrying Moabite women isn't surprising since they are now living in Moab and Israelites were not prohibited from marrying Moabites. On the other hand, Deuteronomy 23:3 forbids Moabites (up to ten generations) from coming into God's assembly. Upon their deaths, Naomi must have felt very alone.

It's said that the only thing worse than losing one's spouse (or parent) is for a parent to experience the death of his/her own child. Parents expect their children to outlive them. This is the normal cycle of life. When the opposite occurs, parents not only feel robbed of their legacy, but they also experience the loss of the future, of their hopes and dreams for their child. Left without a husband and with no sons to help, Naomi had to face the harsh realities of life with only two daughters-in-law.

What kind of hopes and dreams does Naomi have now?

Naomi's story compels us to ask a few questions:

1. Would you have regretted moving from Bethlehem to Moab?
2. How do you think the loss of her husband and two sons impacted her faith?
3. Have you experienced a loss something similar to Naomi?

These tragic experiences occur while Naomi was living away from her redemptive community in Bethlehem. She was far away from her spiritual homeland. So, what makes a redemptive community so unique and special? A redemptive community...

- Reinforces truth and values
- Provides support, encouragement, and accountability
- Helps us to focus on our relationship with God
- Challenges us to be difference-makers in the world

I Will Follow You (1:6–18)

Naomi and her two daughters-in-law might have remained in Moab for several months longer. God, however, sovereignly provided an opportunity for Naomi to return to her redemptive community "for she had heard in the fields of Moab that the LORD had visited his people and given them food" (1:6).

Concerning their return to Bethlehem, a few points are worth asking:

1. Do you think Naomi would have returned to her homeland if God did not provide food in Bethlehem?
2. What is the significance of the narrator calling Bethlehem "home?"

As they were traveling on the road to Judah, Naomi urges her daughters to return to Moab. "Go, return each of you to her mother's house" (1:8). She then blesses them. Her blessings were born out of the hardships of living as a widow with her daughters-in-law. "May the LORD deal kindly with you, as you have dealt with the dead and with me. The LORD grant that you may find rest, each of you in the house of her husband!" (1:8–9)

Because of the loss of her husband and sons, Naomi's words and actions reflect the importance of family relationships. Whereas Bethlehem is home for Naomi, she also mentions how a husband could also be a home for Orpah and Ruth. Naomi's spiritual journey, however, is much larger than just a physical and literal family on earth. God has placed Naomi on a spiritual path that will move her toward finding meaning in a redemptive community.

> God has placed Naomi on a spiritual path that will move her toward finding meaning in a redemptive community.

After exchanging kisses and sharing tears with their mother-in-law, Orpah and Ruth pledge their love for Naomi. "No, we will return with you to your people" (1:10). These women have been through so much together that it was only natural for them to go on with each other. As faithful and loving daughters-in-law, Orpah and Ruth wanted to take care of Naomi.

Did you get the point about *your people* in verse 10? Orpah and Ruth refer to the Israelites as Naomi's people — not their people (Moabites). It's Naomi's redemptive community in Judah that is in view here. Behind the scenes, God has been pursuing Naomi. He is moving Naomi toward her faith community.

Have you been thinking about community lately?
What signs has God placed in your life to nudge you toward community?

Naomi will not have them following her, however. She wants Orpah and Ruth to return to *their home* because Naomi cannot provide a husband or home for them (1:11–13). After weeping once again, Orpah returns to Moab, "but Ruth clung to her" (1:15). Ruth has chosen to remain with Naomi. Naomi attempts to get Ruth to depart again, but to no avail.

Can you imagine this scene played out in front of you?

- Three women kissing and weeping loudly.
- Naomi telling Orpah and Ruth to return home.
- Orpah departs in tears. Naomi then encourages Ruth to go.
- Ruth clings to Naomi's body, tears rolling down both of their faces.
- Finally, Ruth pledges her undying love and support for Naomi.

Ruth was steadfast in her decision to remain with Naomi. Her choice was profoundly moral and highlights her empathy and selflessness. C. S. Lewis observed, "In the moral sphere, every act of justice or charity involves putting ourselves in the other person's place and thus transcending our own competitive particularity."[28] Ruth's promise demonstrated how God's people can partner with Him in the midst of human suffering.

Ruth then pledges her love and support to Naomi. "For where you go I will go, and where you lodge I will lodge. Your people shall be my people, and your God my God" (1:16). What an amazing promise! This is one of the best examples in Scripture depicting covenant love between two people.[29] Ruth's promise to be with Naomi is an amazing pledge.

Let's highlight three ideas:

1. Companionship: Ruth will follow Naomi wherever she goes. She will be a constant and faithful friend to Naomi regardless of the situation. Whether they are rich or poor, happy or sad, strong or weak, Ruth will be there for Naomi.

2. Community: Ruth was a Moabite and she (probably) worshiped the Moabite gods. In the midst of this heart-wrenching circumstance, however, she promises to transfer her allegiance — beliefs, values, lifestyle to the God that Naomi worships and to Naomi's people (Israelites).

3. Commitment: Like husbands and wives who promise to be committed to one another for life, Ruth likewise promises her love and commitment to Naomi. Rather than choosing to be buried with the Moabite people, Ruth's promise extends to being buried in the same place as Naomi.

In summary, a life crisis forces us to consider spiritual issues. Sometimes, we think about the meaning of life and at other times we think about the existence of God. A different crisis might challenge us to reflect on life after death. What we learn here is that...

God has been pursuing both Naomi and Ruth.

Naomi and Ruth's covenant relationship is parallel to God's covenant with His people. In the Old Testament, God established a covenant with Abraham (Genesis 12:1-7), Moses (Deuteronomy 11), and David (2 Samuel 7:8-16). All three of these covenants, however, point to a deeper spiritual reality we have in Jesus. In Jesus's new covenant, our sins have been forgiven and we become members of God's spiritual family.

God is pursuing you. Do you need to take a step towards a spiritual community?

Redemptive Communities Bring Restoration (1:19–22)

"So the two of them went on until they came to Bethlehem" (1:19). What kinds of conversations do you think they had while on the road to Bethlehem? Several topics were probably discussed.

"Naomi, will your people accept me, a Moabite?"

"Ruth, you will surely miss your people in Moab."

"How will our lifestyle in Bethlehem be different?"

"Our God has delivered His people throughout history."

"Naomi, has your God really brought food to His people?"

"Ruth, I will find you a husband."

When they arrived in Bethlehem, the two made quite the impression. As they entered the city, several people stopped what they were doing. Some glanced and others observed carefully. They didn't recognize the younger woman, but the older one looked vaguely familiar. People began to whisper. Then, a few gathered into small groups. Curiosity was in the air. One person said it for everyone:

"Is this Naomi?" (1:19)

You mean the Naomi who…

Left Bethlehem with her husband and two sons.

Has been living in Moab, where false gods are worshiped.

Lost her husband.

Lost both of her sons.

Doesn't have any grandchildren.

Is being accompanied by a Moabite woman.

The older woman of the two looked toward the group. She heard her name spoken aloud (in Hebrew, *Naomi* means "pleasant"). Naomi kept thinking about her name. It would have been easy to simply confirm that she was Naomi — that she was the same person who left several years before. But, she's not the same person. She walked a few more steps with her daughter-in-law, her companion from Moab.

"Do not call me Naomi; call me Mara, for the Almighty has dealt very bitterly with me. I went away full, and the LORD has brought me back empty. Why call me Naomi, when the LORD has testified against me and the Almighty has brought calamity upon me?" (1:20–21)

The word *mara* means "bitter." Acknowledging the lingering wounds that she experienced in Moab, Naomi wants her redemptive community to know that her life is anything but pleasant.

Her life is bitter.

How would you describe your life?

In addition to pursuing Naomi through a redemptive community, God has also been pursuing Naomi as a God of justice. Throughout this narrative, we don't hear too much about God — except that He has taken away, that He has "dealt very bitterly" and "brought calamity" to Naomi. But, we can't forget that God's justice (establishing and upholding the rights of others) includes the idea of restoration and wholeness.

He heard Naomi's cries.

He felt Naomi's pain.

He has perfectly understood Naomi's loss.

So, what is God teaching us through Naomi's life? I think we can learn three things.

1. Knowing our identity begins the process of restoration.

    We can empathize with Naomi's hurt. We can understand why she wants to be called "Mara." On the other hand, perhaps Naomi is also facing her bitterness straight on? Alan Wolfelt in *Understanding Your Grief* explains: "By honoring the presence of your pain, by understanding the appropriateness of your pain, you are committing to facing the pain. You are committing yourself to paying attention to your anguish in ways that allow you to begin to breathe life into your soul again."[30] So, what's Naomi to do?

    In order for Naomi (and us) to take the first steps toward wholeness, it's imperative that Naomi know who she

As Naomi returns to her redemptive community, her identity will be slowly transformed…

is. If we look at things through the lenses of bitterness, then our vision of life becomes a little bit darker. As Naomi returns to her redemptive community, her identity will be slowly transformed from a person of bitterness to a person of service, hope, thanksgiving, security, and blessing.

2. The Lord is the key to our restoration.

Even through her most difficult circumstances, Naomi acknowledges that the Lord was sovereign and in control of the world and her life. While she did proclaim her bitterness, the Scriptures do not give any hint of evidence that she believed that the gods of Moab were in control, that God was too weak (not all-powerful), or that God was too indifferent (not all-loving). Her life of submission and embracing God's plan for her life is the key to restoration.

3. We cannot experience restoration unless we are in community.

Many of us, if placed in similar circumstances, would have cut off our ties from a spiritual community. "I'm not going to church." "I'm not going to that small group." People in spiritual communities are not real, they are not vulnerable, and they don't live in the real world, right? God pursues us through community so that we will ultimately *Go Deeper* with Him. In the midst of our brokenness and heartaches, God wants us to know and experience His passion for us.

John Ortberg notes that "we flourish when we are connected with God and people, and we languish when we are disconnected."[31] Naomi made a decision to return to her redemptive community because it's only here — among people who struggle, who pray, who hurt, who praise, who cry, who persevere — that she can truly experience healing. Her healing will lead to blessing and serving others. Her healing will lead to a grandson. Her healing will (eventually) lead to the praise of God (4:14–15). And why's that?

We were created to live life together.

SUMMARY

1. God has created redemptive communities to assist Him in meeting the needs of suffering people.
2. Redemption includes two ideas:
   - The deliverance from sin based on the payment of Christ's death
   - The deliverance of the whole person — body and soul from suffering and painful conditions
3. Justice (for interpersonal relationships) includes two ideas:
   - The proper and right relationships of people; establishing and upholding the rights of others
   - We should develop God's heart toward the oppressed, hungry, prisoners, blind, humble, alien, fatherless, and widows (Psalm 146:7–9; cf. Deuteronomy 10:17–18)
4. Redemptive communities should be designed to also bring physical and spiritual healing, for both—body and soul.
5. God pursues us through redemptive communities.

REFLECTION

1. What kind of spiritual communities have you participated in before? What were their strengths and shortcomings? How did you contribute to the group?
2. What kind of challenging circumstances have you experienced? How do these experiences encourage (or discourage) you from committing to a faith community?
3. Have you experienced the loss of a loved one? Identify practical ways for grieving the loss of a spouse, parent, child, or friend (choose one).
4. How does helping others to experience redemption and justice relate to the idea of creating a redemptive community?
5. How can faith communities become a place for life transformation? If you were able to create a redemptive community, what traits would it have?

6. We cannot experience true and ultimate healing unless we are participating in a redemptive community. Agree or disagree? Explain.

7. In light of the importance of being part of a redemptive community, how can God use you to pursue your friends, neighbors, and colleagues?

PRAYER FOR SPIRITUAL FORMATION

Dear God,

I am broken. I have experienced pain, suffering and loss like Naomi. But, you are a God of justice. You make crooked paths straight. Father, you make beautiful things. Only you can bring wholeness into fragmented lives. Give me a heart of justice to reach out to the hurting. Help my family, neighbors, and colleagues understand the importance of a spiritual community.

CHAPTER 7

MEPHIBOSHETH
2 Samuel 9:1–12

God's Grace

Introduction

Many of us can recall some of our favorite Christmas or birthday presents. I'm not going to share about all of my favorite gifts, but about one in particular. One Christmas, I received a Yamaha guitar. It came with a hard case too. What a great gift! I learned to play a few chords and even managed to earn a few calluses. Things were going well in the beginning.

However, I had trouble learning the #F chord. It was a bit of a struggle. After a while, frustration began to set in. I practiced less and less. My interest began to wane too. I basically decided to put it down. My guitar has survived a move to Hong Kong and back to California, then to Ithaca, New York, and back to California. The Yamaha guitar wasn't disappointing. My lack of perseverance was disappointing. I still have my guitar. I'm telling you about my guitar because it illustrates

God's grace in our lives. In this introduction, I will share four truths about God's grace.

1. Grace is God's unmerited favor toward us.
    - We are called by the grace of Christ (Galatians 1:6; 1:15).
    - Grace was given to Abraham (Galatians 3:18).
    - We are chosen by grace (Romans 11:5).
    - We receive the riches of God's grace (Ephesians 1:7).

When I received my guitar for Christmas, it was given to me as a gift from my parents. I didn't work for it. I didn't earn the guitar. It had nothing to do with how tall, smart, sporty, or funny I was (or wasn't). Likewise, God's grace has been given to us — we don't deserve it, have not earned it, and cannot do anything to compel God to give it to us. God simply wants to lavish us with His grace. How awesome is that?

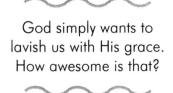

God simply wants to lavish us with His grace. How awesome is that?

2. Jesus uniquely revealed God's grace.
    - God's grace was upon him (Luke 2:40).
    - He was full of grace (John 1:14, 16).

My guitar was a great gift for Christmas! It was shiny and brand new. The guitar revealed my parent's love for me. It uniquely revealed my parents' kindness. In the same way, God sent His Son as a gift to us to demonstrate His love and kindness. Jesus is God's revelation of grace.

3. God's grace in Christ saves us from our sins.
    - Grace that saves (Acts 15:11; Ephesians 2:5; 2:8)
    - Gospel of grace (Acts 20:24)
    - Justified by His grace (Romans 3:24; Titus 3:7; Revelation 1:4)
    - Stand in grace (Romans 5:2)

- Gift of grace (Romans 5:15; Ephesians 3:7)
- Provision of grace (Romans 5:17)
- Grace brings eternal life (Romans 5:21)
- Grace given in Christ (1 Corinthians 1:4; Ephesians 1:6; 2:7; 1 Timothy 1:14; 2 Timothy 1:9)
- Grace reaching more and more people (2 Corinthians 4:15)
- Surpassing grace given (2 Corinthians 9:14)
- Share in God's grace with other Christians (Philippians 1:7)
- Grace of God brings salvation (Titus 2:11)

The purpose of a guitar is to make beautiful music! Although I was an early beginner, I do recall a few good sounds coming out of that guitar. Also, I know the guitar was good because it was used for a few worship services! God's grace in Christ is an unfathomable truth that transcends all thoughts. We're talking about the Incarnation — God becoming human to seek and save those who are lost. A grace that saves is beyond our wildest imaginations!

4. God's grace is sufficient for our entire lives.
    - Stephen, full of God's grace (Acts 6:8)
    - Growing in grace (Acts 13:43; 2 Peter 3:18)
    - Grace in relation to spiritual gifts (Romans 12:6; 1 Peter 4:10)
    - Excel in the grace of giving (2 Corinthians 8:7)
    - Grace abounds to you (2 Corinthians 9:8)
    - Sufficient grace (2 Corinthians 12:9)
    - Conversation full of grace (Colossians 4:6)
    - By His grace, He gave us eternal encouragement and hope (2 Thessalonians 2:16)
    - Be strong in grace that is in Christ (2 Timothy 2:1)
    - We receive grace via God's throne of grace (Hebrews 4:16)
    - We are strengthened by grace (Hebrew 13:9)
    - God gives us more grace (James 4:6)
    - Grace given to the humble (James 4:6)

I was excited when I first began to play the guitar. I could tell I was making progress. I was improving and could see how the guitar could enhance some of my personal times of devotion and worship. Despite these potential benefits, I lost my focus and desire to play. I didn't persevere. I gave up. Growing in God's grace is similar to persevering in guitar playing.

Many of us are initially excited about our relationship with Jesus. We begin to read the Scriptures. We attend church and small groups. We learn about praying to God. We are "on fire" for God. Can you relate to any of this?

Life becomes busy, however. We begin to lose focus and the desire to become all that God wants us to be. We slow down and we choose not to persevere. We become lazy and our passion dies down. In short, we don't grow in God's grace.[32]

But God's grace is sufficient for our entire lives. I want you to know that my guitar still works! It still plays. It still makes good music. In brief, my guitar has been sufficient ever since I received it as a Christmas present.

Background

Before we learn about God's grace through David's kindness toward Mephibosheth, it's important to summarize some of the key events following King Saul's death. The news of Saul's death is met with great sorrow and mourning by David and his followers (2 Samuel 1). David is anointed as king over Judah (2 Samuel 2:1–7). Then fighting between the houses of Saul and David continues (2 Samuel 2:8–4:12).

David becomes Israel's king (2 Samuel 5:1–16) and gains a victory over the Philistines (2 Samuel 5:17–25) and brings the Ark back to Jerusalem (2 Samuel 6). Through Nathan the prophet, David is informed that God will establish a kingdom in his household forever (2 Samuel 7:1–17). David responds in prayer and praise (2 Samuel 7:18–28). God continues to grant David victories over many of his enemies (2 Samuel 8:1–14).

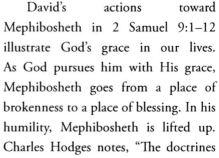

As God pursues him with His grace, Mephibosheth goes from a place of brokenness to a place of blessing.

David's actions toward Mephibosheth in 2 Samuel 9:1–12 illustrate God's grace in our lives. As God pursues him with His grace, Mephibosheth goes from a place of brokenness to a place of blessing. In his humility, Mephibosheth is lifted up. Charles Hodges notes, "The doctrines of grace humble man without degrading him and exalt him without inflating him."[33]

The story of Mephibosheth is a story about God's grace. It illustrates the grace of God found in the life of Jesus. God's grace is significant for many reasons:

1. Salvation is not dependent on gender, appearance, finances, family background, or social relationships.
2. Salvation can't be earned.
3. While salvation is a free gift, it's costly for Jesus (through His death).
4. Proper responses to God's grace include gratitude, peace, joy, worship, and service.
5. God's grace is sufficient for the entire Christian journey.

Grace because of Another (9:1)

In some sense, peace has been restored in the kingdom. When there's peace, we have more time to reflect on life. David was in such a mood. David thought about his relationship with Jonathan, his best friend, who had died in one of the battles after Saul's death.

David inquired, "Is there not still someone of the house of Saul, that I may show the kindness of God to him?" (cf. 9:3). David was recalling how Jonathan (the rightful son to become the next king) had humbly stepped aside for David to be king.

David remembered how Jonathan did not show any jealousy, envy, or hatred toward David, God's choice to be king. His memory would not let him forget that Jonathan protected him from King Saul, who attempted to take his life.

When a new regime came to power, they made sure that the old regime could not take revenge in the future. A simple and brutal way to do this was to take the life of the remaining family members. But David had another idea. Some of his officials were probably thinking, *He's crazy! He's going to show grace to one of the descendants of Saul?*

Brokenness before Grace (9:2–3)

The officials ask a servant of Saul's household, Ziba, to appear before the King. David inquires about the possible existence of a descendant of Saul's. Ziba knows of such a descendant.

"There is still a son of Jonathan; he is crippled in his feet" (9:3).

I don't want to read into Ziba's answer. He's probably just stating a fact: Jonathan's son is crippled. But I don't think it's unreasonable to think that a few of the other officials might have also been throwing around this other idea. "Perfect. Jonathan's son is crippled. He's an easy target for us."

Jonathan's son suffered his crippling injury when he was only five years old. Upon hearing the news of Saul and Jonathan's death, the nurse (who might have been holding him at the time) began to flee, but accidentally fell resulting in a lifelong injury to Jonathan's son (2 Samuel 4:4).

This man experienced a sense of brokenness for most of his life. While he was younger, he couldn't play with the other children. He could only watch them use their feet for walking, jumping, and running. His condition required someone to watch over him as a child. He probably suffered from some social stigma as well. If he was with or near a group of other children, he probably stood out — for all the wrong reasons.

What kind of life was that for King Saul's grandson?

It was a broken life.

Like a shattered vase that has fallen from a shelf, he was broken into pieces.

Grace Finds Us (9:4)

Ziba has a home address for Jonathan's son:

"He is in the house of Machir the son of Ammiel, at Lo-debar" (9:4).

There's some interesting information in this reply. To begin with, the whereabouts of Saul's grandson is known. It's one thing to say that we're aware that Saul has a descendant, but it's quite another thing to inform the king that you know exactly where he lives.

In addition, Jonathan's son is living at someone else's place. Why doesn't Ziba tell David that he simply lives in Lo-debar? Why does he provide the additional information that Jonathan's son "is at the house of Maki son of Ammiel?" Is it possible that Saul's grandson is hiding from David? Does he think that David's going to take his life?

Surrounded by desolation, Jonathan's son needed to be touched by God's hand of mercy.

One other interesting point is that *Lo-debar* has a special meaning. It means "no pasture" (*lo* means "no" and *debar* means "pasture"). Psalm 23 talks about the Lord leading us to green pastures, but Lo-debar was anything but green. Mephibosheth was living in a wilderness — a dry and barren place.

A person living in Lo-debar might have felt like a nobody. Surrounded by desolation, Jonathan's son needed to be touched by God's hand of mercy. He needed to know that he was not beyond the grip of God's grace. Because Ziba knows where Saul's grandson lives, David can be led to this broken person. Even though Jonathan's son is living in a wilderness, David will still be able to find him. Likewise, God knows where you are.

He's pursuing you with His grace.

Perhaps, it's time to stop *hiding* in Lo-debar.

Transformed from the Inside Out (9:5–11)

David sends for Jonathan's son and his servants return with Mephibosheth. What do you think was on Mephibosheth's mind as he moved through the palace? As he looked around, his mind was probably flooded with several thoughts. Here are some possibilities:

1. "Life's not fair. Why am I crippled?"
2. "All of this could've belonged to my father and me."
3. "David doesn't deserve to be here."
4. "I would rather live in the wilderness."
5. "David wants to kill me."

If you were Jonathan's son, what would you have been thinking? As he is brought before David, the king observes the man's face. David could tell that this man had fear. As a gesture of paying honor to the king, the man bows his head to David.

A moment flashes before David's eyes. He remembers Jonathan, this man's father. This broken person is visibly terrified. David speaks:

"Do not fear, for I will show you kindness for the sake of your father Jonathan, and I will restore to you all the land of Saul your father, and you shall eat at my table always" (9:7).

How does Mephibosheth reply?

"What is your servant, that you should show regard for a dead dog such as I?" (9:8).

Mephibostheth has been formed into the image of Lo-debar. He possessed a distorted view of himself (as a dog). Dogs were not looked upon favorably during biblical times. They were considered insignificant. When used of a person, "dog" was a term of scorn or derision. His use of this derogatory title also points to Mephibosheth's view of himself. People who experience low self-esteem and inferiority may also feel:

Inadequate
Unlovable
Depressed
Insecure

How would you feel if you were Mephibosheth?

How can we help people who struggle with low self-esteem and inferiority?

Grace!

God's grace changes Mephibosheth. Grace transforms us from the inside-out. From brokenness to wholeness, God's grace touches us from head to toe — from the inside out. But what good is land if a crippled man can't farm it? David has already considered the issue. He commands Ziba to help Jonathan. "And you and your sons and your servants shall till the land for him and shall bring in the produce, that your master's grandson may have bread to eat" (9:10).

The narrator then leaves the palace scene and the story reaches its climax in 9:11:

"So Mephibosheth ate at David's table, like one of the king's sons" (cf. 9:13).

What an amazing verse! And it's all premised on David's unmerited favor. So, how does grace begin the process of restoration for this broken man? Mephibosheth being adopted into David's family as a son of a king illustrates the deeper truth of our adoption into Jesus's kingly family.[34]

Let me end this chapter with three observations about our spiritual adoption.

1. We have a new identity (son of the king).

    Previously, we were enemies of God, but now we have become friends with Him. Through Jesus, we have been forgiven and reconciled to God. As new creations of God, we are children of God (John 1:12; 2 Corinthians 5:17).

2. We have God's presence and power (living in the palace)

    Previously, we lived in a spiritual desert, but we now live in a king's palace. We were "dead in sin" (slaves to sin), but now alive to God (Romans 6:1–10). As God's temple, the Spirit dwelling in us now empowers us to love God, love others, and make disciples (Matthew 22:37–39; 28:19–20; 1 Corinthians 3:16; Ephesians5:18).

3. God's grace is sufficient for our entire life (land, eating at the table)

Life is full of challenges, twists, and turns. God calls us to persevere and live faithfully. Even though there will be times of doubt, wandering, and weakness, God's grace is sufficient for us (Matthew 6:11; 2 Corinthians 12:9).

SUMMARY

1. God's grace is His unmerited favor toward us. His grace saves us from our sins and can't be earned. We do not deserve God's grace; it's a gift.

2. On the one hand, grace is received freely (by us) but it's also costly (Jesus's life).

3. We are spiritually broken people, but God has been pursuing us with His grace.

4. Grace brings restoration. God heals our brokenness and restores us:

   • New identity
   • Empowerment
   • Sufficient for life

REFLECTION

1. Share about your spiritual journey. What was your worldview growing up?

2. Because God's grace is unmerited favor, we don't have to work, earn, or strive for our salvation. How does this bring peace and freedom in light of our relationship with God?

3. Have you experienced low self-esteem or inferiority? What factors contributed to this view of yourself?

4. Which areas of your life have you experienced God's transforming grace? Which areas still need transforming? Share your experiences with one of your Christian friends.

5. We are taught that God's grace is sufficient for us (2 Corinthians 12:9) and to pray for God's daily bread (Matthew 6:11). How does knowing that God's grace is sufficient for the entire Christian journey encourage you?

6. How does God's grace motivate you for serving others?
7. God has been pursuing our family members, friends, and neighbors with His grace. How can you model God's grace to them? List two or three action points for the next two weeks.

PRAYER FOR SPIRITUAL FORMATION

Dear Father,

You are a God of grace! I am like Mephibosheth. I lived in Lo-debar, a spiritual wasteland. I can't earn or work for my salvation. Salvation is a free gift from you! Help me to see myself for who I really am: beloved and significant. I ask for your daily bread to sustain me. Your grace is sufficient. May I be a source of grace to my family, friends, and neighbors.

CHAPTER 8

ELIJAH
1 Kings 19:1–18

God's Knowledge and Presence

Introduction

"God answered my prayer!" That was all I could think of when it happened. One of the most amazing experiences in life is being a parent. It's also one of the most demanding and challenging as well, especially for first-time parents. For your information, I'm probably the least handy person around. When William was born, however, my handiness was put to the test.

Joyfully put to the test.

There's something about holding a baby in your arms. Even more enduring is holding your very own baby! I remember holding William — you could also carry him like a football with one arm when he was little. Sometimes, however, babies get sick. All parents feel sad when their children get ill. Your heart aches. You feel helpless. You have an enormous amount of compassion and empathy. You just want to be with them when they are feeling miserable. Why?

Our physical presence demonstrates our love, care, and support for one another. When we are physically present, there is a sense of depth that far outweighs a phone call, a Facebook post, or a text message (though sometimes, these are the only things we can do). Because God has created us for community with one another, our physical presence becomes a blessing to others.

William was about a year old at the time when he was really sick. He had a fever. He looked weak and wasn't eating too much. "Ahhh, poor guy...he looks so miserable," I told Peggy. I was also sad because I didn't have an understanding of how William felt. What was William thinking? I wanted to know which part of his body ached the most. I wished I could know William fully when he was so miserable.

It was at this time that I prayed. God answered my prayer — less than a minute later. What happened? William's small body jolted a few times (I was carrying him over my shoulder) and I felt this warm sensation all over my left shoulder. William just threw up! He threw up all over my shoulder! Rather than scream, I felt something totally different.

Satisfaction.
Comfort.
Peace.

Why? Because moments before I had just prayed: "God, I feel so sad for William. Give me his sickness. Let me have his temperature. Give me his hurts. Let me trade places with him. I will do anything to make him feel better."

A few moments later, William tossed his evening feeding onto my shoulder.

Background
My story of a father seeking to know and empathize with his son also illustrates God's omniscience (He is all-knowing) and omnipresence (His

presence is everywhere all the time) in our lives. Although parents lack the knowledge and understanding of their child's thoughts, emotions, and will, God has no such limitations. God is all-knowing. He knows everything completely and perfectly. Nothing catches God by surprise. Scripture attests to God being all-knowing in many ways. He:

- Knows our heart (1 Samuel 16:7; 1 Chronicles 28:9)
- Sees everything we do from heaven (Psalm 33:13–15)
- Knows us intimately (Psalm 139:1–6)
- Is unlimited in understanding (Psalm 147:5)
- Watches both the wicked and good (Proverbs 15:3)
- Is perfect in knowledge (Job 37:16)
- Knows what we do in secret (Matthew 6:4, 18)
- Sees every creature (Hebrews 4:13)
- Knows everything (1 John 3:19–20)[35]

On the one hand, some of us aren't comfortable with the idea that God knows everything about us. But why is that? It is because of the way we live? On the other hand, God's omniscience can help us deepen our faith because He knows everything about us — and yet He still passionately seeks a relationship with us. God's omniscience is important for several reasons:

1. God knows and understands the past, present, and future fully and perfectly.
2. Nothing happens in history or within nature that God doesn't fully and perfectly know and understand.
3. God is not surprised by any of our thoughts, words, and actions.
4. God's judgments are fair because He knows and understands everything.
5. Only God truly knows and understands our pains, hurts, fears, and dreams.
6. God's omniscience can lead to a deeper level of spiritual intimacy.

> Throughout the story, God pursues Elijah to show him the importance of experiencing His presence.

The story of Elijah highlights God's presence, but it also builds on the truth of God's omniscience as well. Because God really knows and understands Elijah, there is a unique opportunity for him to be vulnerable. Throughout the story, God pursues Elijah to show him the importance of experiencing His presence.

Brother Lawrence noted, "The most holy and necessary practice in our spiritual life is the presence of God. That means finding constant pleasure in His divine company…This is especially important in times of temptation, sorrow, separation from God, and even in times of unfaithfulness and sin."[36] Practicing God's presence is not something done haphazardly (even though God is omnipresent). Leading up to 1 Kings, chapter 19, God's presence is demonstrated in Elijah's life in several ways:

- God sends ravens with bread and meat to feed Elijah during a famine (17:1–6).
- God answers Elijah's prayer and raises a widow's son from the dead (17:7–24).
- God teaches Elijah that while He may appear to be absent (Obadiah hid a hundred prophets in two caves), His presence is, nevertheless, always with him (18:1–15).
- God throws fire down from heaven to burn up a water-drenched sacrifice at Mount Carmel (18:16–40). This leads to the judgment of the false prophets of Baal (death by sword).

Running on Empty (19:1–8)

The man who received the message had a look of horror on his face.

"What am I going to do?"

His heart was rapidly beating. He knew one thing for sure. He wasn't going to stick around for the final act.

A crowd of people witnessed his hasty departure. "Where's he going?" "What do we do now?" "What happened?" Someone stepped forward and explained.

"After he led the slaughter of the prophets of Baal, a messenger sent by the Queen Jezebel came looking for him."

Everyone was intrigued. "What did the messenger say?"

The spokesperson cleared his throat: "So may the gods do to me and more also, if I do not make your life as the life of one of them by this time tomorrow" (19:2).

Jezebel had issued a death threat on Elijah. He was afraid. So, with his servant, he ran. And he kept running.

How does fear or other emotions take control of your life?

Where do you go?

Who do you turn to?

Eventually, Elijah arrived in Beersheba in Judah. Then, he went into the desert by himself. Elijah didn't want his servant to accompany him. The prophet wanted to be alone. I'm sure you can relate. Haven't we all wanted to be by ourselves — away from people, noise, work, and responsibilities?

But God is omnipresent. He is everywhere. Because His presence is everywhere, we also know that God will be with us. God wanted to teach the prophet an important lesson:

I'm pursuing you. I know who you are.

You are not alone in my universe.

But Elijah had more than just fear welling up inside him. Elijah was also filled with self-pity and depression. He sat down near a broom tree. He prayed:

"It is enough; now, O LORD, take away my life, for I am no better than my fathers" (19:4).

Did you hear that? This prophet — who ate food carried by ravens, witnessed a dead child returned to life, knew that one hundred prophets were hidden, and saw God send fire down from heaven was ready to quit.

I think Elijah is just like you and me. We have experienced God in many ways. We have seen Him answer our prayers. We know that He's alive. We remember past worship experiences when we felt so intimate and passionate to praise God. We've all been there before.

The question is: Are we there *now?*

What do we do when we are so exhausted?

But, it's more than just being physically tired (he's been traveling through a desert). Elijah was also experiencing depression. Depression comes in many different shades of colors such as a sense of unhappiness, lack of efficiency, distortion of reality, desire to escape, decision to withdraw from people, and thoughts of suicide. Elijah wants out. It's not just out of full-time vocational ministry. He wants to check out of life. Can he feel any lower? Elijah needs rest. He falls asleep.

> Through Elijah, God teaches us a lot about our emotions — the highs and the lows, especially.

Through Elijah, God teaches us a lot about our emotions — the highs and the lows, especially. He also teaches us about weakness as well. We need to find rest when we are physically, emotionally, or spiritually exhausted. We need to slow down. Because He is omniscient, God knows our weakness and how to best support us.

Knowing that Elijah was physically weak, God provided food and water. "And he looked, and behold, there was at his head a cake baked on hot stones and a jar of water" (19:6). Now that's room service!

Elijah might have thought that this was just his imagination. Could those cakes and that water be real? Am I dreaming? Perhaps Elijah was recalling the time when God's presence was manifested when He sent ravens to feed him. At any rate, he ate.

However, Elijah was so exhausted that he fell right back to sleep:

"And he ate and drank and lay down again" (19:6).

I remember experiencing exhaustion like that while serving on a short-term mission trip in Hong Kong. One day we picked up and moved garbage in a squatter's village all morning and then attended a wedding in the afternoon. I couldn't wait to lie down afterward.

Elijah, however, was way beyond this. I'm not sure if we can fully understand his weakened condition. He was thoroughly overwhelmed — physically, emotionally, and spiritually. How do I know? Upon seeing the bread and water, he doesn't even give thanks. There's no "Thank you, God" or "Perfect timing, God!" He just eats and then sleeps.

God again makes His presence known to Elijah by pursing him with the help of an angel.

"And the angel of the LORD came again a second time and touched him and said, 'Arise and eat, for the journey is too great for you'" (19:7).

Life is not easy. Sometimes, we get in over our heads. Left to our own strength, there's no way to get out of our predicament.

But God doesn't leave us alone.

He provides for our needs and strengthens us.

"And he arose and ate and drank, and went in the strength of that food forty days and forty nights to Horeb, the mount of God" (19:8).

God was guiding Elijah to a specific destination. He wanted him to get to Horeb. Without God's strength, he would not be able reach Horeb — God's ultimate destination for him. There he spent the night in a cave.

We need God's guidance in our lives because it's easy to get off His path. Without God's presence to guide him, perhaps Elijah's travel to Horeb would have taken much longer. Am I exaggerating? Because of their sins, the nation of Israel took approximately forty years to reach a destination that should have taken them anywhere from eleven days to a month.

Are you presently on a spiritual journey?

A Gentle Whisper (19:9–14)

Not only in our weakness is God's presence real, but it is also revealed in solitude as well. On the one hand, I'm not saying that we need to go on a forty-day journey into a desert. On the other hand, I'm saying that we need to create times of solitude to focus and listen to God.

Silence is golden.

While in a cave at night, Elijah was spoken to by God:

"What are you doing here, Elijah?" (19:9)

I know what I would have said in response. "What? Are you joking? Why am I here? I'm here because you led me on a forty-day journey. And the reason I went on this journey in the first place was because Queen Jezebel wants me dead."

But Elijah gives a different kind of answer:

"I have been very zealous for the LORD, the God of hosts. For the people of Israel have forsaken your covenant, thrown down your altars, and killed your prophets with the sword, and I, even I only, am left, and they seek my life, to take it away" (19:10).

He doesn't reply to God with a straightforward answer. His answer reveals three things:

1. His passion for obedience: "I have been very zealous for the LORD, the God of hosts."

    What a strong statement! Admittedly, I can't make this kind of statement. What about you? Are you zealous for God and His work? Or are you more zealous for fulfilling your dream of owning a home and moving up the economic and social ladder?

2. His witness (and confrontation) of sin: "The people of Israel have forsaken your covenant, thrown down your altars, and killed your prophets with the sword."

    We are all living in a world that rejects God's beliefs and values, but how do we confront sin? Let me suggest that instead of focusing on a particular sin, we should focus on sharing God's love with a family or a friend. Who are we deepening friendships with so that they will come to know Jesus?

3. His self-pity: "I, even I only, am left."

    Sometimes we feel like we are the only Christians at work or in our neighborhoods. Most of the time, however, this is not true. So what should we do? First, start talking to your neighbors and colleagues! Find out who they are and what they enjoy doing. Invite them over for a meal. Second, connect with your church community, especially the small-group ministry. You'll discover the blessings of giving and receiving love, support, and encouragement.

While part of Elijah's answer might have been correct, I don't think his reply was ultimately what God was looking for. God gives Elijah a specific instruction:

"Go out and stand on the mount before the LORD" (19:11).

Wait a minute! Right here? Right now? Your presence…in your glory… in your holiness…You're going to pass by? Something big is about to happen.

"And behold, the LORD passed by, and a great and strong wind tore the mountains and broke in pieces the rocks before the LORD, but the LORD was not in the wind. And after the wind an earthquake, but the LORD was not in the earthquake. And after the earthquake a fire, but the LORD was not in the fire" (19: 11–12).

So, where was God?

"And after the fire the sound of a low whisper. And when Elijah heard it, he wrapped his face in his cloak and went out and stood at the entrance of the cave" (19:12–13).

While it's true that God's presence can be known in the big things of life, there are times when His presence is experienced deeper in moments of quietness and stillness. But it's more than just being still. God was trying to teach Elijah something.

God spoke to Elijah. He heard God's voice. God's presence will move him to serve. Today, God speaks to us primarily through the Scriptures. Our times of solitude should include God's Word too. We need both solitude and Scripture. While some people create idols out of precious metals or soft clay, many of us bow down to the idol of busyness. Far too often, we go from day to day (and hour to hour) with a list of "things to do." Busy people drown out God's voice.

So, what's the answer?

Slow down.

Stop.

Take a deep breath.

> Busy people drown out God's voice.

Did you know that God has been pursuing you?

What's stopping you from allowing Him to heal your brokenness?

Presence Leads to Service (19:15–18)

Through the life of Elijah, we have learned that God pursues us in our weaknesses. Because He is also omniscient (knows everything completely and perfectly), God understands how to strengthen us when we are emotionally, spiritually, or physically weak and He speaks gentle whispers to our souls. But where does this lead Elijah?

God's presence leads to service.

God tells Elijah to do two things: (1) pronounce judgment and (2) spiritually invest in another person. Sometimes we think that prophets simply made predictions about future events. Their primary role, though, was to reinforce God's covenant with His people and to call them to repentance. Taken in this sense, prophets often served as spokespersons for proclaiming God's holiness. God tells Elijah that several people will be judged (put to death) for their sins.

He also commands Elijah to find Elisha, who will succeed Elijah as God's prophet (see 1 Kings 19:19–21; 2 Kings 1:1–2:18). Elijah's service includes developing a personal relationship with Elisha. He will have to teach and train Elisha to show him what it means to be God's prophet.

Does God have any final words for Elijah? Throughout these chapters, Elijah's key complaint was that he was the only remaining faithful follower of God — he was all alone and no one could understand him. God, however, strongly corrects this opinion. He tells Elijah something special:

"Yet I will leave seven thousand in Israel, all the knees that have not bowed to Baal, and every mouth that has not kissed him" (19:18).

Elijah's way off target. He's off by 6,999! Not only do we learn that Elijah is off with his numbers, but we also learn about God's knowledge and presence in our lives. This is not only a message for Elijah, but it's also a message for us today. What does God want us to know?

He knows us intimately.

We are not alone.

SUMMARY

1. God's omniscience refers to Him as all-knowing. He knows and understands the past, present, and future perfectly and completely. God is not surprised by anything.
2. Because God is all-knowing, He perfectly and completely understands our struggles, pains, sorrow, joy, and dreams.
3. God's omnipresence refers to Him being present everywhere at the same time.
4. When we are weak, God's presence in solitude can be a source of encouragement, support, and strength.
5. Solitude with God leads to serving others.

REFLECTION

1. On a scale of 1–5 (5 being the highest awareness), to what extent have you sensed God's presence in the past month? What are the underlying reasons for your answer?
2. Have you experienced some kind of depression before? What were your circumstances and how did you overcome it?
3. How does God's omniscience (He's all-knowing) encourage you in the midst of a challenging experience? Be specific.
4. How do you practice the presence of God? Share three practical suggestions.
5. What is your strategy for those times when you are physically, emotionally, or spiritually weak? Have you experienced God in a real way during these times? Share your thoughts with someone at your church or in your small group.
6. Why do you think solitude plays such an important role in Elijah's story? How can solitude deepen your own relationship with God?
7. How can practicing the presence of God facilitate a spiritual conversation with one of your friends?

PRAYER FOR SPIRITUAL FORMATION

Dear God,

I want to really know you. I want to experience you in a personal way. Sometimes, you seem distant. Father, you know everything. All of my sins, doubts, and hurts are before you. And...you still love me. I want to experience your presence like Elijah did. In solitude, I wait for you. Reveal yourself to me. Give me strength to share my testimony with my family and friends.

CHAPTER 9

ESTHER
Esther 4:1–9:32

God's Immutability and Faithfulness

Introduction

Are you familiar with Jane Austen's *Sense and Sensibility*? When I was teaching high school literature, I was assigned Austen's book for the student's public exam. The story revolves around the love relationships and personalities of two (different and contrasting) sisters, Elinor and Marianne Dashwood. Elinor is the "sense" and Marianne is the "sensibility" of Austen's book.

In particular, I want to highlight Marianne's two potential suitors: John Willoughby and Colonel Brandon. Willoughby is dashing, fun, exciting, and energetic.[37] We first meet him rescuing Marianne (she sprained her ankle). Thereafter, they spend much time together and they fall in love. One day, however, he informs Marianne that he must attend to business in London and will be away for a season or two.

As providence would have it, the Dashwood sisters have an opportunity to visit London. With great anticipation of seeing Willoughby, Marianne invites him to drop in and visit. Willoughby doesn't reply, however. As chance would have it, they run into him at a party. With callousness, he ignores Marianne throughout the evening. (Later in the story, we learn that he's engaged to a Miss Grey, who is wealthy, worth 50,000 British pounds.)

Eventually, Marianne receives a letter from Willoughby. Perhaps it will help Marianne understand his treatment of her? Will it be an apology? Willoughby informs Marianne that he doesn't have any feelings of romance or love and apologizes for any miscommunication (he also returns her letters and a lock of hair given to him). Marianne is devastated.

Exit Willoughby and enter Colonel Brandon, a friend of the Dashwood sisters. From a literary standpoint, he is the exact antithesis of Willoughby. Brandon is much older and lacks the physical appeal and passion that Willoughby displayed in the earlier part of the novel (read: *boring*).[38] When Brandon first meets Marianne, he immediately falls in love.

In contrast to Willoughby, Colonel Brandon is a picture of faithfulness. In the novel, he is steadfast and faithfully perseveres in his love for Marianne. After Marianne's broken relationship with Willoughby, he comes to visit the sisters in London. In a conversation with Elinor, Brandon divulges what he knows about Willoughby.

Brandon informs Elinor that he was once in love with a lady named Eliza, but they were separated when he went into the army (Eliza then married Brandon's brother). Upon returning from the war, he discovered that Eliza and his brother had divorced and she had had many failed relationships.

As a young lady, Eliza met Willoughby in Bath. From their illicit relationship they have a child out of wedlock. Willoughby, however, abandons Eliza and his child. Brandon visits Eliza on her deathbed and adopts her daughter (who is also) named Eliza. Brandon faithfully raises Eliza from a young age.

Later, in another visit, Brandon informs Elinor that he will give Edward Ferrars (Elinor loves him, but it's complicated!) a place in Delaford. What a gracious friend! The sisters then decide to return home to Barton from

London. Along the way, they stop in Cleveland, where Marianne becomes dreadfully sick. With resolve and perseverance, Brandon faithfully goes to Barton to bring back Mrs. Dashwood to see her ill daughter.

Eventually, Marianne recovers and falls in love with Colonel Brandon. They get married. Brandon's faithful love for Marianne is rewarded. He is trustworthy. He is reliable. In short, Brandon is faithful—his word and actions are true.

Background

When we consider God's faithfulness, we think about God being perfectly and completely trustworthy and dependable. We also relate the idea of God's faithfulness to His ability to keep His promises. How do we know that God keeps His promises? For one thing, many of us have experienced God's promises in our lives (love, joy, peace). In addition, God is faithful because prophesies have come to pass.[39]

We also know that God is faithful to His promises because He does not change. The hymn, "Great Is Thy Faithfulness," highlights this relationship:

Great is Thy faithfulness, O God, my Father.
There is no shadow of turning with Thee.
Thou changest not, Thy compassions, they fail not;
As Thou hast been Thou forever wilt be.

For many things, change can be good because it suggests an improvement or progression. However, "change" for God is bad. If God changes, this suggests that He needs to improve or progress into something better. Peggy and I once took William and Timothy to "see" Plymouth Rock. We were excited. We had high expectations! Do you know what we saw? We saw a tiny rock! The natural elements had changed it.

Like Plymouth Rock, we change through time. Men and women, for instance, make vows (promises) to one another until separated by death. People change their minds and break promises, however. Fifty percent of the marriages in the U.S. end in divorce. On the other hand, since God doesn't change His mind, His promises won't change — He is faithful. In summary, God's immutability (He does not change) plays an important role in relation to His faithfulness.

What does the Bible say about God's immutability? Here are several examples:

- God's nature doesn't change (Psalm 102:26–27; Malachi 3:6; Romans 1:23; Hebrews 1:11–12; James 1:17).
- God's plans stand firm forever (Psalm 33:11).
- God's purposes are always accomplished (Isaiah 46:9–11; Ezekiel 24:14; Hebrews 6:17).
- God doesn't lie or change His mind (Numbers 23:19; 1 Samuel 15:29).
- God is called the Rock (figurative; not subject to change: Genesis 49:24; Deuteronomy 32:4; 1 Samuel 2:2; Psalm 18:31).
- Jesus is the same yesterday, today, and forever (Hebrews 13:8).

God's immutability is proclaimed throughout the Scriptures. What are some implications of God being immutable? J.I. Packer noted: "Where is the sense of distance and difference then between believers in Bible times and ourselves? It is excluded. On what grounds? On the grounds that God does not change. Fellowship with him, trust in His Word, living by faith, standing on the promises of God, are essentially the same realities for us today as they were for the Old and New Testament believers."[40]

Because God does not change, He is perfectly and completely faithful. Because He is faithful, His promises are trustworthy and reliable. There are hundreds of God's promises contained in the Scriptures. The following list highlights "only twenty" promises of God:

- Rest for weary souls (Psalms 23:2; Matthew 11:28–29)
- Restoration of our souls (Psalm 23:3)
- Wait patiently for God and He will hear our cries (Psalm 40:1).
- Trust in God with all our hearts and He will make our paths straight (Proverbs 3:5–6).
- If we wait on the Lord, we will receive strength (Isaiah 40:31).

- A future plan of hope (Jeremiah 29:11)
- We will find God if we search for Him with all of our heart (Jeremiah 29:13).
- When we our weak, God's Spirit intercedes of us (Romans 8:26).
- God causes all things to work together for good (Romans 8:28).
- Nothing can separate us from God's love that is in Jesus (Romans 8:38–39).
- We are God's temple; His Spirit lives within us (1 Corinthians 3:16).
- God's grace is sufficient for us; His power is made perfect in our weakness (1 Corinthians 12:9).
- God can do much more than we can imagine (Ephesians 3:20).
- We can experience God's peace through prayer and thanksgiving (Philippians 4:6–7).
- We can do all things in Christ's power (Philippians 4:13).
- Even when we lack faith, God is faithful (2 Timothy 2:13).
- We receive grace and mercy from God's throne of grace through prayer (Hebrews 4:16).
- If we confess our sins, God cleanses us from all unrighteousness; we experience God's love and forgiveness (1 John 1:9).
- God's perfect love will drive away fear (1 John 4:18).
- One day, all our pain and tears will be wiped away (Revelation 21:4).

What an incredible list of promises given to us by God! Doesn't the truth of God's Word bring assurance, comfort, and peace? Doesn't this lead you to praise and thanksgiving?

The Bible also speaks about God's faithfulness in many ways:

- Abounding in love and faithfulness (Exodus 34:6; Psalm 86:15)
- Faithful in keeping His covenant (Deuteronomy 7:9)
- Called a Rock (Deuteronomy 32:4)
- His ways are loving and faithful (Psalm 25:10).
- The Word is true; He is faithful in all He does (Psalm 33:4).
- Faithfulness reaches to the skies (Psalm 36:5; 57:10)

- Love and faithfulness provide protection (Psalm 61:7)
- Praised for faithfulness (Psalm 71:22)
- Faithfulness surrounds God (Psalm 89:8).
- His faithfulness will be a shield (Psalm 91:4)
- Faithfulness endures forever (Psalm 117:2; 146:6).
- Faithfulness continues through all generations (Psalm 100:5; 119:90).
- Faithful to all His promises (Psalm 145:13; Hebrews 10:23)
- In perfect faithfulness, marvelous things have been done (Isaiah 25:1).
- Messiah: in justice (Isaiah 42:3) (1 Corinthians 1:9); Jesus as great high priest (Hebrews 2:17); faithful witness (Revelation 1:5)
- Faithful to reward and make an everlasting covenant (Isaiah 61:8)
- Great is God's faithfulness (Lamentations 3:23).
- Faithfulness will not allow us to be tempted beyond that which we are able to bear (1 Corinthians 10:13).
- Faithful to secure our salvation (1 Thessalonians 5:24)
- Faithful to strengthen and protect us from the evil one (2 Thessalonians 3:3)
- Faithful even when we are faithless (2 Timothy 2:13)
- Faithful creator (1 Peter 4:19)
- Faithful and just to forgive sins (1 John 1:9)

Because God is faithful, we can trust Him—even in our most difficult experiences.

From these verses, we learn that God's faithfulness covers a broad range of beliefs. Also, some writers used nonliteral language (Rock, reaches to the skies) to describe God's amazing faithfulness.[41] Because God is faithful, we can trust Him—even in our most difficult experiences.

God's faithfulness has also been demonstrated in His relationship with the nation of Israel. In the Old Testament, Israel's history may be summarized in five broad time periods. During these times, we can see God's faithfulness.

1. The Patriarchs: God called Abraham (about 2100 BCE) and promised him as many descendants as stars in the sky. Through Abraham, Isaac, and Jacob, He established the nation of Israel. God's faithfulness was revealed with Isaac, the promised son, and with Joseph's life (Jacob's family moved to Egypt during the famine).

2. Exodus and Wanderings: In Egypt, Israel became slaves for approximately 400 years (ca. 1800–1446 BCE). God's faithfulness was shown in His calling of Moses to liberate His people. He also gave them His Law, but they wandered in the wilderness for forty years due to their disobedience.

3. Settlement and Strife: Under Joshua's leadership, Israel settled in Canaan but did not drive out all her enemies (around 1406–1375 BCE). God's faithfulness was demonstrated by delivering Israel from her enemies despite her lapse into a continuous cycle of sin (from around 1375 to 1055 BCE).

4. Kingdoms: The first three kings of Israel were Saul (1050–1010 BCE), David (1010–970 BCE), and Solomon (970–930 BCE). After Solomon, the kingdom was divided into the northern (930–722 BCE) and southern kingdoms (930–586 BCE). God's faithfulness was exhibited in forgiving the significant moral and spiritual sins of Israel's leaders and establishing an everlasting kingdom through David's ancestry.

5. Exile and Return: Due to sin, Assyria conquered the northern kingdom (722 BCE) and Babylon conquered the southern kingdom (586 BCE).[42] God's faithfulness was demonstrated by protecting His people in exile and by their return to Jerusalem under the leadership of Zerubbabel (538 BCE), Ezra (458 BCE), and Nehemiah (432 BCE). The Old Testament closes with Malachi (ca. 400 BCE).

The Old Testament depicts a God who has been faithful to the nation of Israel. Throughout Israel's history, God has continued to guide, provide, and protect His people. God's faithfulness is significant for many reasons:

1. God's faithfulness encourages trust and a deeper level of spiritual intimacy.
2. God's faithfulness provides peace and hope in the midst of stress, anxiety, insecurity, and fear.
3. Sometimes, God's faithfulness encompasses acts of justice and compassion (e.g., Moses liberating people from Pharaoh).
4. God's faithfulness leads to praise and celebration.

The book of Esther fits into the historical context of the exile period just prior to Ezra's return to Jerusalem. These Jews were living in Susa, the capital city in Persia. They represented a remnant of God's people. God's faithfulness (and sovereignty) was demonstrated by protecting them in light of Esther's decision to plead for her people. The rest of this chapter in *Go Deeper* focuses on Esther 4:1–9:32. The structure of Esther 1–3 may be summarized in four parts:

1. Queen Vashti Vanquished (1:1–22): During a huge banquet for nobles and officials, King Xerxes summons his queen, Vashti. She refuses to come, however. As a result, Vashti loses her crown; she is dismissed.
2. Esther Elected as Queen (2:1–18): In search of a new queen, the King holds a "beauty pageant." Esther, who was adopted by Mordecai (she was the daughter of his uncle), captures the eye of Xerxes. She is crowned the new queen. No one knows that Esther is Jewish because Mordecai tells her to keep her ethnicity a secret.
3. Mordecai Saves King Xerxes (2:19–23): Mordecai overhears a plot to assassinate Xerxes. He tells Esther, who warns the king (she gives credit to Mordecai). Two men are found guilty and hung on the gallows, but Mordecai was not rewarded.

4. Haman's Plan to Terminate the Jews (3:1–15): Haman was given the highest honor of all the nobles for King Xerxes. Everyone was to bow down and honor him, but Mordecai refused. Burning with anger, Haman wanted to kill Mordecai. After learning that Mordecai was a Jew he issues an edict for the destruction of the Jews throughout Xerxes's kingdom.

Sackcloth and Ashes (4:1–4:14)

The sight of the man by the gate was disturbing. He was screaming and weeping. The man's clothes were torn and he was wearing sackcloth and ashes (a sign of mourning).[43]

But it was not only this man.

"And in every province, wherever the king's command and his decree reached, there was great mourning among the Jews, with fasting and weeping and lamenting, and many of them lay in sackcloth and ashes" (4:3).

If placed in a similar situation, how would you show your grief over an edict to destroy your people?

The queen was informed about Mordecai's physical condition (at this time she was not aware of the edict). Esther became "deeply distressed. She sent garments to clothe Mordecai, so that he might take off his sackcloth, but he would not accept them" (4:4).

A change of clothing for his outward appearance would never do justice to the inner grief and pain that Mordecai was feeling. There's a good lesson here: our trust in God's faithfulness will be continuously challenged (e.g., relationships, finances, or health).

Because Mordecai was in sackcloth, he was not permitted to enter the citadel. The queen had Hathach, her attendant, look into the matter. After learning from Mordecai about Haman's plan to annihilate the Jews, Hathach returned with a copy of the edict. Mordecai "command her to go to the king to beg his favor and plead with him on behalf of her people" (4:8).

Esther's first response was somewhat disappointing. She gave Hathach a message to deliver to Mordecai:

"All the king's servants and the people of the king's provinces know that if any man or woman goes to the king inside the inner court without being called, there is but one law—to be put to death, except the one to whom the king holds out the golden scepter so that he may live. But as for me, I have not been called to come in to the king these thirty days" (4:11).

> ...sometimes we need to take more risks and trust Him more because He's already waiting for us to **Go Deeper.**

Although her response reflects the reality of the situation, it simply will not do. It's not good enough. It's not so much that God isn't or won't be faithful to us, but sometimes we need to take more risks and trust Him more because He's already waiting for us to *Go Deeper*.

Mordecai boldly tells Esther (via Hathach):

"'Do not think to yourself that in the king's palace you will escape any more than all the other Jews. For if you keep silent at this time, relief and deliverance will rise for the Jews from another place, but you and your father's house will perish. And who knows whether you have not come to the kingdom for such a time as this?'" (4:13–14)

Every time I read these verses, I either get a chill down my back or a few tears roll down my face. Sometimes, I get both! What about you? What did you think or feel when you read these verses? I love Mordecai's answer! He's proclaiming God's faithfulness! He understands that God has always been faithful to His people — even in the darkest times of their history. It's hard to imagine what must have been going through Mordecai's mind. On the one hand, he was experiencing great sorrow and grief over the edict.

On the other hand, his words also exhibited a deep trust in God's faithfulness. God has always protected His people. The God of Abraham, Isaac, and Jacob is the same God the Jews worshiped in Susa. Regardless of the outcome, there will always be a remnant of God's people who will survive because God's sovereign purposes will be fulfilled.

The Risk Taker (4:15–5:8)

Mordecai's message was received loud and clear. Prior to these verses, we are only given a small glimpse of Esther. Esther's second reply to Mordecai allows her character to shine. What does she say? Let me share two observations.

1. "Go, gather all the Jews to be found in Susa, and hold a fast on my behalf, and do not eat or drink for three days, night or day. I and my young women will also fast as you do" (4:16).

What a godly woman! If it was me, I probably would have just run into the palace and gone straight to the king. I would have looked at my iPhone and said I have no time to waste. I need to see the king.

How would you have handled the situation?

Esther calls for the whole Jewish nation in Susa to fast! Fasting was one of the spiritual disciplines God's people used to deepen their passion for God. Rather than feasting on food, fasting encourages us to hunger for God. Fasting is usually accompanied with prayer (and/or worship) and reveals our brokenness before God. Although the text doesn't say it, I'm quite confident that the Jews in Susa also combined prayers with their fasting.

There's another issue worth exploring here as well. Although Esther is a Jew, she's been living in the palace away from her people. (Recall that she wasn't aware of the edict.) The palace walls not only physically separated her from her fellow Jews, but it also acted as barrier between God and herself. In short, God has been faithfully pursuing Esther, but the walls of the palace have kept her away from Him.

God has been faithfully pursuing Esther, but the walls of the palace have kept her away from Him.

Like Esther, God has been faithfully pursuing you.
Have you also built walls to keep Him away?

2. "Then I will go to the king, though it is against the law, and if I perish, I perish" (4:16).

Esther's determined to not approach the king until after they have fasted. Esther's priority for fasting highlights another principle of trusting in God's faithfulness. Although God faithfully pursues us, we are responsible for responding to Him. God always has the first word and we have the second. He speaks first; we reply second. Throughout the story, God has been calling out to Esther. In calling for a fast, Esther was responding to God's faithfulness.

God has been calling out to you, too.

How will you respond to His faithfulness?

By approaching the king, she knows that she may die ("if I perish, I perish"). But she lays it all on the line. This is why we love Esther! Perhaps, if she stayed quiet, she might escape the edict (I know what Mordecai said but she is the queen after all). Regardless, Esther knows that God is faithful (and sovereign too).

On the third day, Esther was "standing in the court" and the king held out "the golden scepter that was in his hand" (5:1–2). Reflecting on this episode in Esther's life, Charles Swindoll highlights the impact of fasting and prayer on her moment of truth: "Esther walks in…confidence. Look at her. She doesn't cringe and cower; she stands…She's not trembling. Though she's doing what's never been done before, she is standing tall, confident in the Lord."[44]

Enthralled with his queen, the king promised Esther anything up to half the kingdom. She invites the king to attend a banquet that she has prepared for Haman. A second time, the king promises her up to half the kingdom, but Esther defers and asks for them to return the next day for another banquet.

In the Line of Fire (5:9–9:32)

The rest of the story of Esther may be summarized in four parts. (1) Chapter 5:9–14: Haman and his wife invited some friends over for dinner. Reveling in his pride, he explained how he was honored above all and was invited by Queen Esther to return the following day. Haman was still fuming over Mordecai, who refused to bow down to him. Haman's friends encourage him to have a gallows built to hang Mordecai. Haman agrees. Mordecai probably went to sleep with a smile.

(2) Chapter 6: Browsing through the chronicles, the king discovers that Mordecai uncovered an assassination plot, but was not rewarded. Wanting to reward Mordecai, he asks Haman indirectly what should be done for such a man. Haman thinks that the king wanted to honor him so he tells the king that this person should be honored among all the people. To Haman's shock and anger, Mordecai is paraded through the streets with a royal robe and horse. Haman goes home seething. Before anything else can be done, however, he is whisked away to the banquet.

(3) Chapter 7: In the middle of the banquet, the king again asks Esther what she wishes for. Esther tells him that she and her people will "be destroyed...killed.... annihilated" (7:4). The king is upset. Asking for the identity of such an evil person, Esther replies that it's Haman. Using the very gallows that he had built to hang Mordecai, Haman himself meets his death.

(4) Chapters 8–9: Because the edict cannot be reversed, the king writes another one in behalf of the Jews that "allowed the Jews who were in every city to gather and defend their lives, to destroy, to kill, and to annihilate any armed force of any people or province that might attack them, children and women included, and to plunder their goods" (8:11).

Chapter 9 highlights the fighting between the Jews and the other provinces and cities. Following the original edict, their enemies wanted to destroy them, but the Jews soundly defeated them. With the defeat of their enemies, they celebrated with great joy. As a result, the feast of Purim has become a celebration of God's faithfulness to the nation of Israel.

Many of us have been jaded from life experiences. Most of us can recall when someone—a politician, manager, coach, teacher, family member, or friend let us down. That moment was like air being leaked out of a balloon. The story of Esther, on the other hand, reminds us that we trust God because He will always be faithful.

SUMMARY

1. Because God is faithful, He is trustworthy and dependable.
2. God's immutability (He does not change) is related to His faithfulness. God is immutable in the following ways:
   - God's nature doesn't change.
   - God's plans stand firm forever.
   - God's purposes are always accomplished.
   - God doesn't lie or change His mind.
   - God is called the Rock (figurative; not subject to change).
   - Jesus is the same yesterday, today, and forever.
3. God's faithfulness has been demonstrated in His promises to us (see the list of twenty above).
4. God's faithfulness has also been demonstrated by establishing, nurturing, and protecting the nation of Israel.
5. At times, we may think or feel that God has not been faithfully pursuing us because we have not yet taken the risk to *Go Deeper*.

REFLECTION

1. Can you recall a time when you experienced God's faithfulness in your life?
2. How does knowing that God doesn't change (He's immutable) encourage your relationship with Him? Be specific.
3. Read the list of God's twenty promises again. Select three promises and explain their significance in your life with one of your Christian friends.
4. How does a Christian community play a role in assisting us to experience God's faithfulness?
5. What risk is God asking you to consider? (Depending on the risk, you may want to share it with another person for accountability.)
6. God is still faithfully pursuing your family and friends. He has not given up hope. Sometimes, however, our desire for sharing our faith lessens. List three suggestions for faithfully pursuing our families and friends.

PRAYER FOR SPIRITUAL FORMATION

Dear Father,

You are a faithful God. Everything around me changes, but you don't change. Even when I lack faith, you remain faithful. I trust you because you keep all of your promises. Sometimes, I don't feel confident when you ask me to take risks. Like Esther, I want to trust you. Help me to take risks this week to share the gospel with my family or friends.

CHAPTER 10

PRODIGAL SONS
Luke 15:11–32

God's Love

Introduction

The word "love" has been quoted in some of the most iconic sayings throughout history. The idea of love is found in literature, songs, and all forms of culture. Here's a small sampling:

- Samuel Butler: "It is better to have loved and lost than never to have loved at all."
- *Love Story* (movie): "Love means never having to say you're sorry."
- John Lennon and Paul McCartney: "All you need is love."
- Zelda Fitzgerald: "Nobody has ever measured, even poets, how much love a heart can hold."
- Martin Luther King, Jr.: "There can be no deep disappointment where there is not deep love."

- William Shakespeare: "The course of true love never did run smooth."
- Mother Teresa: "Love is a fruit in season at all times, and within reach of every hand."
- Ice-T: "Passion makes the world go round. Loves just makes it a safer place."
- Elizabeth Barrett Browning: "How do I love thee? Let me count the ways."
- Leo Tolstoy: "All, everything that I understand, I understand only because I love."
- Helen Keller: "The best and most beautiful things in the world cannot be seen or even touched. They must be felt with the heart."

When it comes to love, everyone has their opinion about what love is and what love isn't. Love is one of those words that's hard to define, but many believe they know it when they see it and experience it. What about you? How would you define love?

Background

If we are to understand the depth of the father's love depicted in Jesus's parable of the lost sons, then we need to discover what the Bible teaches about God's love. The Bible declares that "God is love" (1 John 4:8). God's essence, His very character is love. John 3:16 is a good place to learn about God's love.

Besides Genesis 1:1, John 3:16 might be the most popular verse in the Bible. It's one of the first verses many Christians memorize after they become followers of Jesus Christ. It's so well known that we're not surprised to see people holding JOHN 3:16 signs and banners during NFL football games.

What makes this verse so popular? For one thing, it's the message of the gospel in one verse: "For God so loved the world, that he gave his only Son, that whoever believes in him should not perish but have eternal life." In addition, John 3:16 is a window into God's heart of love. From John 3:16, I have identified five aspects of God's love.

1. *For God so loved the world*

    God's love is passionate. God's love is seeking, an otherness kind of love that pursues and follows. It's active and dynamic and not a static kind of love that God possesses. God's love desires, feels, and moves.

2. *That he gave*

    God's love is sacrificial. God's love is not self-centered. It's not a selfish kind of love that thinks only of Himself. Rather, it's a giving-of-oneself kind of love that was given for the world. God's sacrificial love has been demonstrated by sending Jesus to the cross.

3. *His only Son*

    God's love is unique. The Greek word *monogenes* means "unique, one of a kind." God's love is special and incomparable to other forms of love (e.g., a wife's love for her husband, a parent's love for their children, and friends' love for one another) because His love involves His unique, one-of-a-kind son, Jesus.

4. *That whoever believes in him*

    God's love is inclusive. While it's true that salvation is in Christ alone (John 14:6; Acts 4:12), the path is inclusive because the gospel saves people regardless of their ethnicity, gender, social status, or financial means. God's love invites everyone to hear the good news found in Jesus Christ, who came to seek and save the lost.

5. *Should not perish but have eternal life*

    God's love is everlasting. God's love is not whimsical; it's not hot one day and cold the next. God's love doesn't change because of circumstances. God's love is an everlasting kind of love because it's found in Jesus. In Christ, you are loved forever — nothing can separate you from God's love found in Christ (Romans 8:38).

The word "love" appears in 684 different verses. The Bible declares God's love from beginning to end. Scripture highlights God's love in many different ways:

- God keeps His covenant love (Deuteronomy 7:9, 12; Nehemiah 1:5; Dan 9:4)
- Steadfast love (Psalm 33:5; 33:18; 51:1; 52:8; 77:8; 107:8, 15, 21, 31; Lamentations 3:22)
- Great is His love toward us (Psalm 117:2)
- Love endures forever (1 Chronicles 16:34; 2 Chronicles 5:13; 7:3; 7:6; 20:21; Psalm 100:5; 106:1; 107:1; 136:2)
- Redeemed in his love (and pity) (Isaiah 63:9)
- God's love poured out into our hearts by the Spirit (Romans 5:5)
- God's love demonstrated by Christ's death for us (Romans 5:8)
- Nothing can separate us from God's love in Christ (Romans 8:38-39)
- God has great love for us (Ephesians 2:4)
- We are beloved, dearly loved by God (Colossians 3:12)
- Loved us through His grace (2 Thessalonians 2:16)
- Prayer: direct our hearts to God's love (2 Thessalonians 3:5)
- Love made prefect when we obey His Word (1 John 2:5)
- Love comes from God (1 John 4:7)
- Love demonstrated by sending Jesus (1 John 4:9, 10)
- God's Love made perfected when we love each other (1 John 4:12)
- Keep ourselves in God's love (Jude 1:21)

God's love doesn't get old and His love doesn't get tired, bored, or lonely. It's a passionate love. It's love in action! God's love is important for many reasons:

1. God is love; God Himself, His very character is love.
2. In contrast to the world of self-centeredness, God's love is passionate, sacrificial, unique, inclusive, and everlasting.
3. God's love is demonstrated by His sending Jesus to die on the cross for our sins.
4. God's love is found in Jesus.
5. Because He is love, God wants to bless us.

6. Knowing and experiencing God's love brings security and
    significance.

When Love Was Not Enough (15:11–12)

A man had two sons. They had different temperaments and outlooks on
life. The older son was hard-working, diligent, and sought to win his father's
approval by doing the right things. He was very dutiful, generally keeping
his thoughts private. The younger son was less diligent and probably more
carefree and spontaneous. He was the more relaxed brother of the two and
(eventually) sought to live apart from his father's love.

Which brother are you more like?

How has your *personality* affected your relationship with your father
or mother?

This story (Luke 15:11–32) has been commonly known as "The Prodigal
Son." Perhaps, you've heard of it? (I refer to this parable as "Sons" because
both sons are spiritually lost.) As a response to some of the religious leaders
who were criticizing him for eating with "sinners," Jesus tells them three
parables (Lost Sheep, Lost Coin, Lost Son). All these parables illustrate one
key theme:

God pursues us with His love and celebrates our return home.

Have you been *away* from God?

Where is *home* for you?

Do you long to find your *place* in this world?

Let's continue with Jesus's parable about the lost sons. One day the
younger son decided he wanted something more out of life. Maybe he was
bored doing chores and working in the fields? Knowing that his father was
pretty wealthy, he demanded his money:

"Father, give me the share of property that is coming to me" (15:12).

Although this was not a common request during this time, it wouldn't
necessarily be out of the question either. According to custom, the older
son would receive two-thirds and the younger son one-third of the wealth.

So, the Father gave the younger son his inheritance. Case closed.
"Here's your money, son. You're an adult. Do whatever you want, but
choose wisely."

We need to ask a few questions before we continue with the story:

1. If the father loved the younger son, why did the son want to leave?
2. Can we reach a place in our lives when love is not enough?
3. What should we do when the ones we love don't want to be loved?

Running from God's Love (15:13–19)

So the younger son did…whatever he wanted. He packed his bags. Actually the text says that he "gathered all he had" (15:13). Not only was he preparing to run away from his father's love, but he had no intention of returning. By taking everything he had, the younger son was saying that he was going to find a new home. He didn't want to leave any of his belongings because he wasn't coming back.

When you were younger, did you ever threaten one of your parents with the classic, "I'm packing my bags and leaving home for good" power-play? We did this because we wanted our parents to shout out, "I love you!" Or we wanted our parents to feel guilty or sad for something. We thought that our impending departure would give us control over the situation.

Maybe the younger son wanted more control over his life. He was thinking of making a permanent change. He was taking things to the extreme. He was going to go far away from his father's home.

But God pursues us with His love.

We can never outrun God's love for us.

He had money to burn — places to go and people to see. Living carelessly, he eventually spent all his money on "reckless living." In order to understand this story better, we'll place the younger son's actions in our time and culture. So here are some things the younger son might have done today:

- Gambling (and losing) on sports, cards, or other games
- Purchasing expensive clothes
- Buying the latest tech gadgets
- Ordering the finest foods and drinks
- Hosting parties and treating others

- Initiating improper relationships
- Creating an entourage for social partying

His money eventually ran out. He was in a jam. Perhaps, his new friends could help him? Maybe they could find him a temporary job or something. The parable says nothing about friends. These so-called friends probably just hung around while the younger son had money. As soon the money ran dry, his entourage also disappeared.

The younger son has…

No money.
No job.
No family.
No friends.

Now, what should he do? Is returning home an option?
Would you go home?
Not yet, anyway. The younger son landed a job feeding pigs in a field. It was a humble job. To make matters worse, there was also a famine in the area. Life was becoming more desperate for him.

"And he was longing to be fed with the pods that the pigs ate, and no one gave him anything" (15:16).

The younger son needed to find a better job. "Will work for food" was what his sign said. The son became homeless, emotionally broken, and hungry.

I want to interject something here. Because Jesus is using this parable to illustrate a spiritual truth, I want to suggest that the younger son's predicament — homeless, broke, and hungry — illustrates our spiritual condition as well.

> …the younger son's predicament — homeless, broke, and hungry — illustrates our spiritual condition as well.

We are spiritually homeless, broken, and hungry when we live apart from our heavenly Father's love.

In addition, the younger son was experiencing guilt over his decisions. First, he rejected and ran away from his father's love. Second, he lived recklessly and immorally. What could the younger son do? How should he deal with guilt? In *Life's Healing Choices*, John Baker, highlights five principles for "moving past guilt" in light of a person's overall process of spiritual recovery:

1. Take a personal moral inventory.
2. Accept responsibility for your faults.
3. Ask God for forgiveness.
4. Admit faults to another person.
5. Accept God's forgiveness and forgive yourself.[45]

These five principles illustrate the younger son's choice to return home. He hit rock bottom. His life had now spiraled out of control. Circumstances forced him to do some soul searching. After some time, the younger son (finally) came to his senses:

"My father's servants are better off than me. I will return home and confess my foolishness to him. I don't deserve to be his son, but will ask him to hire me as a servant."

So, the son takes off…

He's (finally) returning home.

Although he was still a long way off, he was probably becoming anxious.

"Has my father been thinking of me?"

"What will my father say?"

"Does my father still love me?"

"Will he reject me?"

The Father's Love (15:20–24)

Frank A. Clark noted, "A baby is born with a need to be loved and never outgrows it."[46] Regardless of where he had been or what he had been doing, the younger son still needed his father's love. While the parable highlights the idea of the younger son wanting to return home due to a lack of food,

I am also convinced that he returned home because he longed to be with his father as well.

What about you?

Have you outgrown your need for love?

Jesus has been telling this story with the spotlight on the younger son. You might be wondering, "What's going on at home while the younger son was wasting his money?" Jesus now brings the Father and older son into the story.

"But while he was still a long way off, his father saw him and felt compassion, and ran and embraced him and kissed him" (15:20).

Did you get all of that? Now that's love in action!

Let me share three observations from this description of the father.

1.   The father was out looking for his son to return.

     This is the passionate kind of love that I mentioned previously. The father was probably on the porch looking to see if the next person coming onto the estate was his son. He wasn't sitting out back on some old rocking chair squashing spiders.

2.   The father was filled with compassion for his son.

     There's no hint of condemnation or seething judgment. We get the impression that we're not going to get the "It's about time" or "I told you so" speech from this father. The father's compassion is a deep-seated emotion.

3.   The father ran to his son; he hugs and kisses him.

     Can you sense his excitement? He couldn't wait to shower him with his love. He didn't wait for his son to arrive at their home. Rather, the father ran to greet and welcome his son home. What a passionate father! What an amazing father! What a forgiving father!

But wait, the father's not finished…

Probably wiping away the tears from his eyes and visibly shaken and overcome with emotion, the father announces to all the workers on the estate, "Bring the best robe. Put a ring on his finger. Give my son sandals.

We're going to eat some prime rib. We're having a celebration. Let's get the music going. We're going to be dancing all night long."

I have three words for you:

Best.
Father.
Ever.

The younger son had already decided that he was undeserving to be a son. He wanted to be a hired servant. His father desired a passionate relationship with his son. The younger son must have been so overwhelmed with tears and emotions. This is what love can do. Passionate love reconciles broken families. Passionate love melts the most callous hearts. The wayward, rebellious son has returned home. He's ready to begin a new relationship with his father. So, it's all good, right?

Working for Love (15:25–32)

There's still another son. Having worked all day, the older son approaches home. He's probably tired for putting in a full day's work. On his "things to do" list he has completed eight-five percent of it. Covered by the dust and dirt from working on the estate, he continues his slow and methodical steps as he gets within earshot of the family's home.

He whispers under his breath:

"I hear music and see dancing." Being a person of order, he's wondering…

"What's going on here?"

"What's this celebration all about?"

"Why didn't I know about this party?"

One of the servants comes out to meet the older son. Then, he explains the situation to him. The servant tells him about his younger brother finally returning home after all these months. The servant can't even finish the whole story because the older son refuses to listen to it. He abruptly leaves the conversation.

How would you have felt if you were the older son?

The older son is *now* livid. He refuses to step inside. He walks several feet away from the house. Filled with jealousy, rage, and bitterness, he will not acknowledge his brother's existence.

What kind of relationship do you think he had with his father? Robert McGee in *The Search of Significance* observes, "Our self-concept is determined not only by how we view ourselves but by how we think others perceive us. Basing our self-worth on what we believe others think of us causes us to become addicted to their approval."[47]

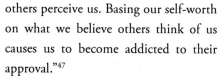

Rather than freely receiving his father's love, he sought it through doing good works and living an ethical life.

The older son longed for his father's approval. Feeling good about himself was directly related to being accepted by his father. His way of gaining his father's love was fulfilling his duties around the estate. Rather than freely receiving his father's love, he sought it through doing good works and living an ethical life.

What kind of relationship do you have with your heavenly father?

The servant who shared the good news with the older brother enters the home. He sees the father laughing and having a wonderful time. It's a celebration! His younger son has returned home! Not wishing to be the bearer of bad news, the servant needs to inform the father about the older son.

Immediately, his father comes outside. He's looking for the older son. Upon finding him, he doesn't lay down the law. Filled with compassion, he pleads with the older son to come inside to welcome his brother back home. The father explains to his overwhelming joy and gratitude about his brother being found.

"I thought your younger brother might be dead. I waited and waited every day for his return. Every time I passed by his empty room, I was crushed and my heart ached beyond measure. I wanted your brother to come home. And now he has."

The older son can't believe what's he's hearing. He tries to hold his tongue, out of respect for his father, but after a minute or so, he just lets it all out:

"I've been faithful all these years. I did everything you wanted. Why didn't you give me a celebration? Now, when this wicked son of yours returns from the dead, you forgive him and throw him a party. He wasted his money on wild living. You're not fair! Why don't you love me as much as him?"

If you were the father, what would you do? How would you respond to this angry son? The father says two things:

1. "Son, you are always with me, and all that is mine is yours" (15:31).

    In other words, your very life is a blessing to me. I'm so grateful for you. You have always been my son. That will never change. I will always love you. Nothing will separate you from my love. Look around. What do you see? What's mine is yours. You don't have to work for these blessings. You freely receive this because you are my son.

2. "It was fitting to celebrate and be glad, for this your brother was dead, and is alive; he was lost, and is found" (15:32).

    Life is too precious and sacred. It's said that one of the great tragedies of life is the death of a child before his or her parent. But this son is alive! This celebration doesn't mean that I have not been thinking of you. You have always been on my mind and in my heart, son. We need to celebrate because your brother has (finally) found his way home.

If you were the older brother, how would you have felt?
Some things are just worth repeating:

Best.
Father.
Ever.

It's easy to read this story and highlight the younger brother's condition. He needs to return home. All of us need to return to our Father. However, we need to remember the older brother, too. He shows us that having a relationship with the Father (God) is not about doing the right things. The older son wanted the father's approval. Having a relationship with God is not about "working" for God's love, however. The older son also shows us that being a "good" person isn't the same as having a relationship with our Father.

It's about God's pursuing us with His love.

An intimate, spiritual relationship with God is based on a personal relationship with Jesus, His Son. The older son's disappointment points us to Jesus, who came to reconcile us to the Father.

What about you? Perhaps, you have been on a spiritual journey for the past several weeks, months, or years. You think you've been doing all the right things. You've been climbing this spiritual mountain — more meditation, more discipline, and more good works.

God, our heavenly Father, is ready to celebrate and throw a party for you — one that is filled with food, music, and dancing.

But you're missing one thing. What is this *one* thing?

Your heavenly Father passionately loves you. He wants to have a relationship with you. He's waiting with open arms for you to return home.

God has been pursuing you with His love.

And when you return home...

God, our heavenly Father, is ready to celebrate and throw a party for you — one that is filled with food, music, and dancing.

SUMMARY

1. God's love is radically different from any other kind of love that we have experienced. God's love is passionate, sacrificial, unique, inclusive, and everlasting.

2. Because God is love, He wants to bless us (life, talents, relationships, food). However, the ultimate expression of God's love is demonstrated by sending Jesus to die for our sins.

3. Some of us are like the younger brother — we believe that God's love is not enough. We have chosen to live independently from Him.

4. Some of us are like the older brother — we work for God's approval and try to do the right things in order to be accepted by Him. We feel that being a moral person is good enough.

5. God pursues us with His love and celebrates our return home.

REFLECTION

1. Reflect on your spiritual journey. Has it been more like the younger or older son? Both? Explain.

2. The younger son represents our desire to live apart from God. (This person doesn't necessarily have to be financially poor or immoral. Most are the opposite.) How do you have spiritual conversations with "younger sons"?

3. The older son represents the person trying to "do the right things" for God's approval. He is also the kind of person who believes that being a moral person is good enough. Share a few suggestions for sharing your faith with "older sons."

4. What are some characteristics of the Father revealed in this story? How can these characteristics encourage you to deepen your relationship with Him?

5. Take time this week to show God's love to someone who doesn't have a relationship with Him. Share about this experience with someone at your church or in your small group.

PRAYER FOR SPIRITUAL FORMATION

Dear God,

I know that you love me, but sometimes I don't feel it. Like the young son, I want to live apart from your love. Sometimes, I feel like the older son...I do things for your approval. Father, help me to experience your love and acceptance. Nothing can separate me from your love in Jesus. Empower me so that I can show your love to my family and friends.

CONCLUSION

For parents of newborns, holding their baby is one of life's most treasured and amazing moments. As you wrap your arms around this small, fragile, sweet baby — your joy overflows. Your heart is overcome with emotions. I have been blessed with these kinds of experiences with my two sons. Perhaps, a similar experience will occur if I become a grandparent?

Looking back at my time as a father of newborns — my sons were born two-and-a-half years apart — I enjoyed this stage of parenting. It wasn't easy — there was a lot of crying from those two boys, much diaper changing and less sleeping for my wife and me, but it was worthwhile and life-changing. I recall communicating in "baby talk" with my boys.

During this baby stage, however, I also wanted my sons to be able to understand my words and express their thoughts and feelings. I wanted to show them the beauty of the world. I looked forward with anticipation to my son's physical, intellectual, social, and spiritual development (Luke 2:52). But why is that? I think it's because we want to see our children grow and mature. This is what *Go Deeper* is all about.

When a lost sheep has been rescued, a lost coin is found, or prodigal sons return home, there is great rejoicing in heaven (Luke 15:5–7, 9–10, 22–32). When we become children of God (John 1:12), our Father wants to develop a dynamic and intimate relationship with us. God, our heavenly Father, wants to see us, His children, grow and mature.

God wants us to *Go Deeper* with Him. But what does this mean? Not only does He take the initiative to reveal Himself and save us, but God is also proactive in deepening His relationship with us. He's not just waiting for us. God is actively seeking us — He's relentless in His pursuit.

> He's not just waiting for us. God is actively seeking us — He's relentless in His pursuit.

While it's true that I need to do my part in the relationship — read the Word, pray to God, worship, and be in community with other Christ-followers, and serve — it's important for me to understand that God has been pursuing me throughout my spiritual formation. This is one of the most profound truths I have ever discovered.

At their foundation, the stories in *Go Deeper* proclaim a God who pursues us with His holiness, grace, sovereignty, and faithfulness. We come to know more of God and understand the kind of God He really is. In addition, I believe there are four other reasons why God pursues us:

1. God pursues us because He has a plan for us (Jeremiah 29:11). We have a role to play in God's metanarrative.
2. God pursues us because He wants to transform us into the image of His Son (Romans 8:29). The goal is not simply salvation, but to develop Christ's character in us.
3. God pursues us so that we can impact others. As salt and light (Matthew 5:13-16), we reach out to connect with and serve others with acts of compassion and justice.
4. God pursues us in order to bring satisfaction and fulfillment to our lives (John 10:10). To truly live for God — to know and experience Him — is to find meaning in life.

From my understanding, to *Go Deeper* with God implies that He wants to *Go Deeper* with us. Taken in this sense, *Go Deeper* establishes a foundation for spiritual formation. So how do we build upon this foundation? We need to understand how the Spirit forms us — the intentional process by which the Spirit develops Christ's character. In short, the next level — part two in this series — will focus on the developmental process of becoming more like Christ.

ABOUT THE AUTHOR

Ken Jung (PhD, University of Bristol, England) is Pastor of Spiritual Formation at Bridges Community Church. Having served in multicultural churches for over ten years (US, overseas), Ken has also been an adjunct teacher in theology, religion, and philosophy. *Go Deeper* combines his love for theology and literature. One of Ken's passions in life includes training national pastors and leaders. Visit Ken's blog, *Renewing Eli*, a site dedicated to his writings on spiritual formation. Ken lives in Fremont, California, with his wife and two children.

THE NAMES OF GOD

Names are very important in the Scriptures. In general, many names were chosen because they had a special meaning. More importantly, names often represented a characteristic associated with a particular person. In Scripture, God has many different names. The names of God represent the many different attributes of God's nature.[48]

Yahweh	The Self-Existent One (Exodus 3:14–15)
Yahweh Yireh	Lord will provide (Genesis 22:8–14)
Yahweh Shalom	Lord is peace (Judges 6:24)
Yahweh Sabbaoth	Lord of hosts/armies (Psalm 24:10)
Yahweh Raah	Lord is my shepherd (Psalm 23:1)
Yahweh Tsidkenu	Lord our righteousness (Jeremiah 23:6)
Yahweh Rapha	Lord who heals (Exodus 15:26)
Yahweh Elohim	Lord, the Mighty One (Judges 5:3)
Adonai	Lord (Joshua 7:8–11)
Elohim	Mighty One (Genesis 1:1)
El Elyon	Strongest, Mighty One (Genesis 14:18)

El Shaddai	Almighty God (Genesis 17:1–20)
El Olam	Everlasting God (Genesis 21:33)
El Elohe Israel	The God of Israel (Genesis 33:20)

ENDNOTES

1   Genesis 2:7, "then the LORD God formed the man of dust from the ground [body] and breathed into his nostrils the breath of life [spirit], and the man became a living creature [soul]." The idea of a "soul" (total person) is generally different than the "spirit" (life that empowers). It's important to note, however, that Scripture uses these words in different ways. For example, David asks God for a renewed "spirit" to relate to God (Psalm 51:10). "Body" can refer to our whole person (Romans 12:1) and "spiritual body" (1 Corinthians 15:44) refers to our future resurrected and glorified body. In Isaiah 10:18, "soul" and "body" depict the whole person and Jesus teaches that the "soul" survives death while the "body" cannot (Matthew 10:28). See Robert L. Saucy, "Theology of Human Nature" in J. P. Moreland and David M. Ciocchi, eds., *Christian Perspectives on Being Human* (Grand Rapids: Baker Books, 1993), pp. 17-52.

2   A. W. Tozer, *The Knowledge of the Holy* (San Francisco: Harper & Row Publishers, 1961), p. 19. In addition to the attributes highlighted in *Go Deeper*, Tozer's book includes God's self-existence, self-sufficiency, wisdom, transcendence, and goodness.

3   Drawing insights from the book of Daniel, J. I. Packer in *Knowing God* identifies four characteristics of people who know their God: (1) they

have great energy for God; (2) they have great thoughts of God; (3) they show great boldness for God; (4) they have great contentment in God (London: Hodder and Stoughton, 1993), pp. 27-33. To Packer's list, I would also add transformation (fruit of the Spirit: Galatians 5:22-23).

4   See Larry W. Hurtado, *At the Origins of Christian Worship* (Grand Rapids, MI: William B. Eerdmans Publishing, 2000), pp. 63–97. In Revelation 5, the Apostle John highlights the worship of the Lamb of God (Jesus). In John's vision of worship, Jesus receives the same glory, honor, and praise as the Father, who is seated on the throne (Revelation 4).

5   The words found in Deuteronomy 6:4–6 are known as the *Shema*. It was Israel's affirmation of faith in the one and true God. He alone created the universe, bringing order from chaos, redeemed them from Pharaoh's bondage, sustained them during their comings and goings, and will one day establish a new heavens and earth.

6   A list of spiritual gifts from Romans 12:6–8; 1 Corinthians 12:8–10, 28, and 1 Peter 4:11 include prophecy, serving, teaching, encouragement, contribution, leadership, mercy, wisdom, knowledge, faith, healing, miracles, distinguishing spirits, speaking in tongues, interpreting tongues, helps, administration, and speaking.

7   From my perspective, story theology is similar, but different from narrative theology. A theological movement during the late 20th century drawing from the writings of Hans Wilhelm Frei, George Lindbeck, and Stanley Hauerwas, narrative theology has become popular among the emergent church movement. We may summarize narrative theology with three key points. First, narrative theology believes that the biblical narratives represent theology rather than the propositions of faith found in systematic theology. Second, narrative theology believes that biblical propositions are dependent on narratives for their meaning. Narratives have priority and not the doctrines. Third, narrative theology calls the Church to know and live out the story in light of their social contexts (family, work, school, community).

I have five reasons why I prefer to use the term "story theology" rather than "narrative theology." First, narrative theology is generally critical toward systematic theology, but I see systematic theology in a more positive light. Second, narrative theology may undermine the objective interpretation of the text by focusing on the reader's interpretation of the story. On the other hand, I believe that Scripture has one correct and objective interpretation with many applications. Third, narrative theology may fail to consider the historical context for interpreting the text when emphasizing the reader's application to the stories. In each chapter of this book, I provide a historical background for each character to help us interpret the story.

Fourth, narrative theology may limit the use and application of principles because it highlights the person's relationship to the story. While understanding our life in light of the story is a good starting point for understanding the text, we do people a disservice if we don't help them practice and live out the text as well. Fifth, present day use of the term "narrative theology" is usually associated with the emergent church movement.

For critical observations about the emergent church, see D. A. Carson, *Becoming Conversant with the Emerging Church* (Grand Rapids: Zondervan, 2005) and Kevin DeYoung and Ted Kluck, *Why We're Not Emergent* (Chicago: Moody Publishers, 2008). For a general introduction to story theology, see C. S. Song, *In the Beginning Were Stories, Not Text* (Cambridge, UK: James Clarke & Company, 2011). Song has many good insights, but I part ways in light of his theology of pluralism. I wrote a review of Song's work in *Reviews in Religion and Theology*, Vol. 20, Issue 2, pp. 323-326.

8   Chip Ingram, *God* (Grand Rapids: Baker Books, 2004), p. 32. In this book, Ingram writes about the importance of seeing God for who He really is and highlights His goodness, sovereignty, holiness, wisdom, justice, love, and faithfulness.

9   The Big Bang is the term used to describe the origin and development of our universe. Many scientists believe the world came into existence approximately 13.7 billion years ago. My discussion with John highlights

what has been traditionally referred to as the "cosmological argument" (cosmos means "world"). In brief, the cosmological argument attempts to show that it's reasonable to believe that the universe was caused by an eternal creator.

10 According to deism, God created the world (He might be all-powerful) and life, but has probably deserted us. The God of deism is transcendent (above and beyond) but not immanent (up close and personal).

11 I used this scientific/philosophical approach with John because he believed that Genesis 1 contradicted science.

12 Jeshurun is a poetic term used to describe the nation of Israel.

13 In addition to the literal twenty-four hour interpretation of Genesis 1, there are other views concerning the meaning of "days" such as aeons (long time periods), literary-framework (poetical in nature: day 1, 2, 3 are parallel to days 4, 5, 6), and appearance of age.

14 Henry van Dyke's "Joyful, Joyful, We Adore Thee" depicts how creation reflects God's majesty and leads us to praise.

> All Thy works with joy surround Thee,
> Earth and heaven reflect Thy rays,
> Stars and angels sing around Thee,
> Center of unbroken praise;
> Field and forest, vale and mountain,
> Blossoming meadow, flashing sea,
> Chanting bird, and flowing fountain
> Call us to rejoice in Thee

15 Martin Luther, *An Open Letter to the Christian Nobility* (1530): "A cobbler, a smith, a farmer, each has the work and office of his trade, and yet they are all alike consecrated priests and bishops, and every one by means of his own work or office must benefit and serve every other, that in this way many kinds of work may be done for the bodily and spiritual welfare of the community, even as all the members of the body serve one another."

16 See Robert S. McGee, *The Search for Significance*, Revised and Expanded (Nashville: Word Publishing, 1998), pp. 111-121.

17 Saint Sister Faustina, *Diary*, p. 180. Faustina's *Diary*, written in the style of a journal, contemplates the soul's union with God.

18 Benjamin Franklin, The Constitutional Convention, July 28, 1787.

19 John Piper, *Desiring God*, 10ᵗʰ Anniversary Expanded Edition (Sisters: Multnomah Publishers, 1996), p. 222.

20 Joni Eareckson Tada, *Is God Really in Control?* (self-published, 1990).

21 Rudolph Otto, *The Idea of the Holy* (Oxford: Oxford University Press, 1950), p. 12. Otto's book summarizes his findings about how people from different cultures act when experiencing someone/something that they believe to be "holy." According to Otto, this *mysterium tremendum* can be manifested in several way such as a "gentle tide," "set and lasting attitude of the soul," "burst in sudden eruption up from the depths of the soul," "wild and demonic forms," "crude barbaric antecedents and early manifestations," "something beautiful and pure and glorious," or "bushed, trembling, and speechless humility." (pp. 12-13)

22 Jonathan Edwards, *President Edwards*, Volume V (New York: G. & C. & H Carvil, 1830), p. 143; citing Jonathan Edwards, *On Religious Affections*.

23 John Piper, *Let the Nations Be Glad!* (Grand Rapids: Baker Books, 1993), p. 11.

24 There are several ways to address the issue of evil and suffering in the world. First, concerning the idea of running the universe, this question implies that this person has more knowledge and wisdom than God because they have a better plan or know how to balance the issues of human freedom, humanity's selfishness, justice, love, etc. Second, this view suggests that because evil is not yet destroyed then God cannot or will not destroy it. If God is all-powerful and all-loving, then God can and will defeat evil in the future.

    Third, God created human beings with the capacity to sin or not to sin. The presence of evil in the world is due to the free will of humans and consequences of the fall. Thus, God is indirectly but not directly responsible for the origin of human evil. Although this is not the best world (the new heavens and earth will be the best), it's the best way to the best world (allowing humans the free will to choose, mature, develop character, persevere, etc.). Fourth, if God was to destroy evil today, then Jesus would be returning to judge humanity. God's decision to *not* wipe out evil (and to do so yesterday, for instance) may also be interpreted as a sign of His mercy — God is providing more opportunity for people to repent and be saved.

Fifth, although evil and suffering appear to be senseless, there are a many reasons God allows some evil and suffering to occur, including (1) judgment, (2) reality of sin, (3) a testimony to the brevity of life, and (4) a means of glorifying God. Sixth, God's reply to evil and suffering was to send the Messiah, who is Jesus. Jesus's death and resurrection paves the way for defeating evil in four ways, including: (1) transformed and glorified bodies, (2) freedom from the bondage of sin, (3) the defeat of Satan, and (4) the future re-creation of the world. Seventh, God, our Father, can empathize with us because He knows how it feels to lose a son. He had to witness His Son's brutal death. He knows what it feels like to see an innocent victim suffer and die at the hands of evil perpetrators.

25 See Timothy Keller, *Generous Justice* (New York: Dutton, 2010), pp. 1–18.

26 Ibid., p. 3.

27 See H. Norman Wright, *Crisis Counseling*, Updated and Expanded (Ventura: Regal Books, 1993), pp. 151-179.

28 C. S. Lewis, *An Experiment in Criticism* (Cambridge: Cambridge University Press, 1969), p. 138.

29 The relationship between Jonathan and David is another example of a covenant friendship (1 Samuel 20:1–42).

30 Alan D. Wolfelt, *Understanding Your Grief* (Fort Collins: Companion, 2003), p. 15.

31 John Ortberg, *The Me I Want to Be* (Grand Rapids: Zondervan, 2010), p. 185. Ortberg further explains how a lack of community can impact a person negatively: "Emotionally, isolated people are more prone to depression, anxiety, loneliness, low self-esteem, substance abuse, sexual addiction, and difficulties with eating and sleeping." (ibid)

32 The significance of God's grace for our lives is demonstrated with Paul's greetings in grace (Romans 1:7; 1 Corinthians 1:3; 2 Corinthians 1:2; Galatians 1:3; Ephesians 1:2; Philippians 1:2; Colossians 1:2; 1 Thessalonians 1:1; 2 Thessalonians 1:2; 1 Timothy 1:2; 2 Timothy 1:2; Titus 1:4; Philemon 1:3; 2 John 1:3) and farewells in grace (Romans 16:20; 1 Corinthians 16:23; 2 Corinthians 13:14; Galatians 6:18; Ephesians 6:24; Philippians 4:23; Colossians 4:18; 1 Thessalonians 5:28; 2 Thessalonians 3:18; 1 Timothy 6:21; 2 Timothy 4:22; Titus 3:15; Philemon 1:25).

33 Josiah H. Gilbert citing Charles Hodges in *Dictionary of Burning Words of Brilliant Writers* (New York: W. B. Ketham, 1895), p. 334.

34 When David was on the run from Absalom, he met Ziba. He inquired of Ziba about the whereabouts of Mephibosheth. Ziba informed David that he remained in Jerusalem awaiting the return of his father's throne. Feeling betrayed by Mephibosheth, David takes back the lands and gives them to Ziba (2 Samuel 16:1-4). Later, however, Mephibosheth claims that Ziba lied about him (Mephibosheth has the physical appearance of someone who had been mourning). Consequently, David orders Mephibosheth and Ziba to divide the lands between them (2 Samuel 19:24-30). These transpiring events do not nullify the initial teaching about God's grace (2 Samuel 9:1-12). Rather, they illustrate how grace can be given by an imperfect and sinful person (David) as opposed to a perfect and righteous God (Ephesians 2:8-9).

35 This view of God's omniscience (classical theism) rejects open theism. Open theists maintain that God cannot exhaustively know the future. Rather, God knows only that which can be knowable. Since the future is unknown, then it follows that God cannot exhaustively know the future. Key advocates for open theism include Gregory Boyd, Clark Pinnock, and John Sanders.

36 Brother Lawrence, *The Practice of the Presence of God*, Abridged Version (Springdale: Whitaker House, 1982), p. 59.

37 His description in Jane Austen's *Sense and Sensibility*: "Willoughby was a young man of good abilities, quick imagination, lively spirits, and open, affectionate manners. He was exactly formed to engage

Marianne's heart; for, with all this, he joined not only a captivating person, but a natural ardour of mind…" (London: Penguin Books, 1995), p. 46.

38 According to Willoughby, "Brandon is just the kind of man whom everybody speaks well of and nobody cares about; whom all are delighted to see and nobody remembers to talk to" (p. 48).

39 Several Messianic prophesies, for instance, have been fulfilled in Jesus including Genesis 3:15, 49:10; 2 Samuel 7:16; Psalm 2:7; Micah 5:2; Isaiah 9:1–2, 9:6, 11:10, 53, and 61:1–2.

40 Packer, *Knowing God*, p. 89.

41 Concerning the significance of God's faithfulness, A.W. Tozer in *The Knowledge of the Holy* stated, "Upon God's faithfulness rests our whole hope of future blessedness. Only as He is faithful will His covenants stand and His promises be honored. Only as we have complete assurance that He is faithful may we live in peace and look forward with assurance to the life to come" (p. 132).

42 After the northern kingdom is conquered, they disappear from the Bible. The southern kingdom in exile (e.g., the book of Daniel) and the return of a remnant of God's people to Jerusalem (e.g., the books of Ezra, Nehemiah) becomes the focus of the redemptive story line.

43 Context determines the meaning. Wearing sackcloth and ashes could also be a sign of repentance.

44 Charles R. Swindoll, *Esther* (Nashville: W Publishing Book, 1997), p. 101.

45 John Baker, *Life's Healing Choices* (New York: Howard Books, 2007), pp. 106-114.

46 Frank A. Clark (1911-1991) was an author and cartoonist for *The Country Parson*.

47 McGee, *The Search for Significance*, p. 61.

48 This is a partial listing taken from H. Wayne House, *Charts of Christian Theology and Doctrine* (Grand Rapids: Zondervan Publishing House, 1992), pp. 51–52. For my list, I have used the word "Lord" rather than "Yahweh."

CPSIA information can be obtained at www.ICGtesting.com
Printed in the USA
BVOW08s0826151113

336275BV00002B/5/P